THE FIRST 130 FEET

True Stories from the Dive Deck

Ken Barrick

iUniverse, Inc.
Bloomington

The First 130 Feet
True Stories from the Dive Deck

iUniverse books may be ordered through booksellers or by contacting:

iUniverse
1663 Liberty Drive
Bloomington, IN 47403
www.iuniverse.com
1-800-Authors (1-800-288-4677)

ISBN: 978-1-4620-6302-4 (sc)
ISBN: 978-1-4620-6304-8 (hc)
ISBN: 978-1-4620-6303-1 (e)

Printed in the United States of America

iUniverse rev. date: 10/24/2011

CONTENTS

The stories contained herein are true and factual events.
Most last names have been omitted and in some cases
first names have been changed. In some cases boat names
have also been changed or eliminated altogether.

Author – Ken Barrick
Editor – Philip DePalo
Assistant Editor – Michelle Barrick

A DVD Video companion to this book is available for purchase.
The DVD contains actual footage of events mentioned in this
book, including a shark sneezing, a shark walking backward
using its' pectoral fins, the sea lion kiss and more. To purchase
the DVD, please visit my website at www.kbdiverservices.net
or, fill out the form located in the back of the book and mail to:
KB Diver Services, PO Box 24814, Middle River MD 21220.

PREFACE

The thing I enjoy most about SCUBA diving is sharing my passion with others. As a SCUBA Instructor I have an opportunity to share this passion on a regular basis. With that in mind; writing this book gives me the opportunity to share my passion with a much larger group of people.

The story of how I became a diver isn't glamorous but it is interesting. I met my wife Michelle at the TGI Friday's® in Towson, Maryland. It was a blind date and I had high hopes for that evening. When I first laid eyes on her, I was instantly attracted. Things were going well and through conversation I learned that Michelle was a SCUBA diver. She made it very clear that if I wanted to continue dating her, I'd have to become a diver too. It was her intention to travel the world, and I'd have to be game for anything.

We continued dating and not long into the relationship she surprised me with a gift, the SSI Open Water SCUBA Diver course from Aqua Ventures in Cockeysville, Maryland. I was thrilled but apprehensive. While this had always been a dream of mine, it may not have become a reality if Michelle hadn't come into my life. I will forever owe her for this blessing.

Learning to dive in the late 1990's was challenging. The sport of recreational SCUBA diving was still very much in its infancy and while a few hardy souls had begun diving regularly in the 1960's the sport was hardly mainstream and still today only about one percent of the U.S. population is certified to dive. The percentage of certified divers in many countries is even lower, but there are also countless numbers of uncertified divers throughout the world.

Improvements in everything from training to equipment and even breathing gases have been dramatic over the past thirty years. Enriched Air Nitrox (EAN) was just becoming accepted in recreational diving during the late 1990's and training agencies were still working toward standardization. Things such as recommended depth limits and dive table development for Open Water SCUBA certification were being debated and changed due to litigation concerns.

SCUBA diving was considered an extreme sport during the 1990's and in some circles it still is. It was stressed throughout my class that I could die if I didn't follow the rules. On average, people who learn to SCUBA dive participate in the sport for just a short time . The reasons for quitting the sport are many. One reason is that parents of young children fear dying and leaving their children alone. A second is that many older folks (60+ years of age) enter the sport, and after a few years, their health deteriorates.

Learning to dive was one of the few things in life that gave me a sense of fulfillment. It ranks just behind showering and brushing my teeth as something I've done longest in my life. I've now been diving more than fourteen years, and I still have a strong desire to discover new locations and aquatic life. Michelle has been diving for twenty years and is still passionate about it.

In 2002 I made SCUBA diving my business. I started a company focused on providing underwater services to recreational boaters. It didn't take long for KB Diver Services to become one of the most active underwater businesses in Baltimore.

In 2003 I decided to become a SCUBA Instructor. I added educational courses to my business offerings and actively teach private SCUBA lessons.

Now, here I am in 2011 writing down some of the memorable moments in my diving career. They are all interesting stories. Those of you who dive will find stories similar to your own. Those of you don't will hopefully find stories that motivate you to get certified. I've always had a simple philosophy about life; there are only three places human beings have a chance to explore in their lifetimes, the land, the sea and outer space. Most of us will never get the chance to reach outer space, but all of us have the chance to reach the ocean floor. With more than seventy percent of the earth covered in water, how much life will you miss if you don't take the plunge?

I hope that you enjoy these stories and perhaps even learn a thing or two. These stories are my passion and I am very happy to share them with you.

Ken Barrick

GETTING HAMMERED

I was awakened by the bright sun, the beams crossing my eyes through the window of my room at the Riding Rock Inn. It was all the motivation I needed to jump to my feet and start the day. I peered out the window to a gorgeous sunrise. Here I was, getting set for my first morning of diving in San Salvador.

The first stop was breakfast with my dive group. There were sixteen of us. Many in the group were highly experienced divers, a few were once a year vacation divers and there was one girl taking her very first dive trip after being certified back in Baltimore.

Breakfast for the most part seemed uneventful as our large group dined together discussing the upcoming morning dives. The only thing of importance I noticed was one young man in our group, seemingly in his early twenties was pouring something from a flask into his orange juice. He seemed to be doing it discreetly, keeping it from view of the group leader. I didn't know the young man and despite my misgivings, I decided to mind my own business and keep the information to myself. I was not about to get into a riff, with a total stranger, on the very first morning of the trip.

After breakfast my wife and I scurried to our room, collected our dive gear and headed down to the boat. We set up our dive gear and watched as the others set up theirs. Being a dive-master at the time, I could tell who was comfortable and competent and who may end up needing assistance by observing how they assembled their gear and how much fidgeting they were doing afterward. This seemed like a tight, well trained group. I noted quick assembly of gear, all the while joking with no signs of stress or anxiety. I decided to take a seat and enjoy the sun beating down on me. We had clear skies, sunshine, warm clear water and a great group of divers. What more could I want on a dive vacation?

As we approached the first dive site we were advised it was a swim-through, in essence a hole or cut in the reef that acted as a tunnel for us to dive through. The dive briefing informed us that as we swam through the cut, we would come to a Y. At this juncture it was preferable to stay to the right and by doing so we would come out of the reef and onto the wall in about 90 feet of water. The passageway on the left was narrow, fully enclosed and would bring us out on the wall 130 feet below. We could follow the resort dive master Ray or we could go it alone. For those who were not interested in doing the swim-through, they could glide over the top of the wall and stay at a comfortable depth. We could expect to see friendly groupers, a variety of reef fish and hammerhead sharks. This was, after all, San Salvador, famous for hammerhead shark encounters.

Despite being an experienced diver, I am not known to push the limits. My wife and I had listened to the briefing and decided we would dive the swim-through and turn right, the more conservative option bringing us out on the wall at 90 feet. We geared up along with everyone else and splashed in as a large group. Ray motioned for everyone to follow him. As we tagged along I spent some time observing everyone in the water, noting that the entire group seemed to have above average buoyancy control and smooth kicking strokes. I thought to myself, this was going to be an excellent week of diving.

Upon arriving at the entrance to the swim-through, Ray stopped and pointed to the opening. Instead of leading us through, he would hover above on the wall and make sure everyone made it in and out of the swim-through okay. If he led us, he would be turning his back to us and would lose sight of everyone. His plan made perfect sense.

The most excited to enter was our freshly minted diver Allison. This was her first open ocean dive and she made it clear she wanted to be first into the swim-through. I remember thinking to myself as she entered, "I'm not so sure this is the best idea, a brand new diver going first into an enclosed space." If she panicked she would cause a back-up in the tunnel and we could all end up in a world of trouble.

Allison entered first followed by Joe the young man I had observed adding pep to his orange juice at breakfast. I took it upon myself to wedge myself into third position, figuring if trouble ensued, I may be one of the better people in the group to handle it. My wife Michelle tucked in behind me.

With my adrenaline pumping and senses on high alert I squeezed myself through the narrow swim-through, thrilled that the two divers in front of me were not impeding my progress. Visibility was not the best, it was dark and those before me had stirred up just a bit of sediment. I reached the Y and instinctively followed the fins in front of me to the left, forgetting in that moment my plan to go right. There was no turning back now.

Everything happened so fast. I saw a massive shape making a u-turn and Allison using her arms to propel herself backward. It was a 14 foot Great Hammerhead, turning and using its massive head to bump Allison backward... nudging her in her chest, one bump, then two, then three. From the corner of my eye I saw Joe snapping pictures with his camera and then my hearing senses kicked in and I heard "clang, clang, clang." I looked around then up and saw Ray frantically motioning for everyone to ascend. I looked at my depth gauge and it read 135 feet. I looked back at Allison and observed one last nudge from the shark before it turned and continued on its way, leaving Allison stunned but intact and Joe with amazing photographs.

The four of us, the only members of the group who turned left at the Y, slowly ascended to meet up with Ray and the rest of the divers. After everyone in the group used the okay sign to ask Allison if she was in fact okay, we swam to the top of the wall at 50 feet and met up with some friendly Grouper.

The Grouper, just like the shark, also took an interest in Allison and I began to wonder if this girl was a mermaid with magical powers over the fish in the sea. My wonder was soon explained when Joe and his friend Mike swam over to Allison, opened her BCD pockets and began pulling out breakfast sausages.

Not known to me or anyone else in the group, including Allison, her two prankster friends had placed a multitude of breakfast sausages in her BCD. They later explained to us why they had done this. On one of their previous diving trips, they had learned that Grouper loved breakfast sausage. Their intention was for Allison to be swarmed by the friendly, harmless Grouper, making this an amazing first dive experience. They had not planned on the passing senses of a 14 foot Great Hammerhead. The shark apparently smelled the sausages in her BCD and came in to check it out. Lucky for Allison, Joe, Mike and the rest of our group, the Hammerhead decided not to take a bite.

At dinner, Ray made us all say a pledge out loud, "NO MORE PRANKS." He had been completely spooked by the actions of the Hammerhead, saying he had been diving in San Sal for a long time and had never observed a Hammerhead approach a diver like that. For her part, Allison was thrilled. She thought the entire experience was awesome. We were quick to tell her she may have just had the most amazing experience she will ever have in diving and all on her very first dive.

LEAP OF FAITH

Roatan, Honduras is one of my favorite places to dive. The plunging walls host an abundance of life, from fish to black coral and everything in between. There is something for everyone visiting this underwater realm.

This dive day began like many others. Our group boarded the boat and headed out for what was supposed to be a fantastic wall dive. The captain planned to position the boat on top of the wall; the dive master would then enter and lead our group to the dive's starting point approximately forty feet below. We were all comfortable with the plan; there was nothing unusual about it. It should have been a straightforward dive.

The last thing I do before I jump off a perfectly good boat is take a compass heading in the direction of my intended destination. As I approach my entry, I ask the captain or dive master to point in the direction of my intended target. Wherever they point, I take a compass heading directly to that spot. Depending on their professional knowledge is a small leap of faith that has never steered me wrong. If I enter the water into a worst case scenario, such as poor visibility or no visual reference points, I am able to competently navigate forward until something comes into view.

As an Instructor, I always teach my students to take a reciprocal course heading. This is a simple out and back course beginning where they enter the water. On this trip none of my students were diving with me. Michelle, me, and the rest of our highly experienced group would be following the resort dive master.

The plan started off without a hitch. The boat captain indicated to the dive master that we were in position, the dive master gave the signal and one by one we did our giant stride entries into the clear blue water. The dive master gave the signal for our group to begin descending and down we went.

The visibility was very good. By all accounts we had close to one-hundred feet of visibility or better. Due to the excellent visibility I was confused. As we descended I could not see the top of the wall. It was supposed to be just forty feet below. The dive master was leading and I was at the tail end of the group; a position I often take up to ensure that everyone is doing okay.

I kept watching the group ahead of me. All I could see was blue water in all directions. There was no wall in sight. I finally decided to look at my depth gauge and it showed 100 feet. I realized something wasn't right. We were not on the wall, not even close. I looked forward and observed the resort dive master spinning in circles and motioning for everyone to ascend. My gauge now showed 110 feet.

Roatan has many walls that are sheer drop offs into the abyss. The wall we were diving on reportedly dropped to more than one thousand feet. It would have been very easy for us to get into serious trouble. Spatial disorientation is a major problem for divers in clear blue water. With no visual reference points, there were now thirteen of us in this very precarious situation.

I exerted myself quite a bit in an effort to pass the rest of the group and reach the dive master's position. I got her attention, picked up my compass and acquired the heading I had set prior to jumping off the boat. I motioned for the dive master and the rest of the group to follow me. Apparently neither the dive master nor anyone else in our group had taken a compass heading prior to jumping off the boat. She looked at me quizzically but fell in line behind me. My only worry now was – had the Captain actually pointed me in the right direction? With this worry in the back of my mind, I ascended to seventy feet and stayed on my heading. It seemed like I was swimming for an eternity and I was just about to give up and lead the group to the surface when the massive wall appeared ahead of me. Oh how glorious it was. If you've ever had the chance to swim from blue water onto a wall, you know what I mean.

For those of you who have not had such an opportunity, picture being able to fly like a bird and soaring toward the side of a mountain. The visual impact is the same. I could look down the wall into the abyss... and I could look up to see the sun's rays coming over the top of the wall. The colors popped as I approached the wall. I could see schools of fish swimming in formation around coral heads and sea fans. This is a view very few recreational divers will ever see.

I glanced at my computer and it showed I had been in the water a total of twelve minutes. Most of those minutes were a blue water swim I will never forget. The anxiety of being in blue water, one hundred feet beneath the surface, with the realization that there were nearly one thousand more feet beneath me; it took my breath away. The pride I took in leading my comrades out of the blue and back to the wall was priceless. To this day many of them still talk about this dive and the amazing view it afforded them.

Personally, I still consider every jump from a perfectly good boat a "leap of faith," and after this one in blue water, I no longer place any faith in resort dive masters. I approach each and every dive as if it is me against the world. I have faith in the ability of three people to get me back to the boat – me, myself and I.

I listened intently as the dive master and boat captain debated who was at fault for the predicament. Did the captain drop us in the wrong place? Did the dive master somehow begin her initial descent in the wrong direction, leading us away from the wall? I will never know for sure, but I do know that this dive ranks among my all-time favorite dives and I told them both they should take credit for that!

LOST AT SEA

Diving from a live-aboard dive boat, basically a small floating resort on the water has become one of my passions. Having traveled extensively around the world diving from these types of vessels from the Bahamas to Australia, I have come to appreciate the added sense of adventure. There is nothing quite like the feeling of standing on the forward deck peering out into an endless expanse of water, with no land in sight. You come to feel the sense of adventure Jacque Cousteau must have felt exploring the worlds' oceans.

On this morning I would be diving with a close knit group of friends on the sailing vessel *Domino* out of Miami Florida. We had been at sea for a couple of days and the diving had been wonderful and uneventful. Our dives had included typical encounters with reef fish, turtles, moray eels and the like. The crew seemed more than capable and our group of experienced divers was in the process of lulling them to sleep. The crew had little to worry about as we repeatedly entered and exited the water without incident.

The next dive on a site named Triple Sevens would change all that. Tim and Mary were both experienced divers, but didn't dive on a regular basis. They were your annual vacationers, doing fifteen or twenty dives a year. They had looked smooth on all of our dives to date, so I had no concerns as we entered the water. The planned dive seemed easy enough. It was only 60 feet to the sandy bottom and the plan was to follow the anchor line forward to a set of shallow pinnacles, small pyramid shaped reefs sticking up out of the sand.

I was the first to enter the water and I was instantly met with a moderate current. The current was running from bow to stern and the boat was holding position with the anchor line headed straight into the current. The visibility was okay but not great. I'd later estimate it to be 30 to 40 feet. As I descended, around 20 feet or so, I was kicking forward to the anchor line when I looked back at my wife and noticed she was getting nowhere. It was as if she was kicking in place, making no forward progress at all. As the thought popped into my head that perhaps we should abort the dive, she signaled to me that she was descending to the bottom. I glimpsed at the anchor line, set my compass on a direct heading to the line and descended with her. When we reached the bottom, the current dissipated and we made our way across the sand using my compass heading. Eventually we came to one of the pinnacles and located the anchor. Remembering the visual image of the site from the dive briefing, I felt confident we could navigate the site and end up back at the anchor line.

We set out diving around the pinnacles and eventually came across the rest of the divers. Everyone seemed to be doing fine. A total of twelve divers had entered the water and it seemed all were present and accounted for. Further proof, I remember thinking to myself, that this was a well rounded and experienced group.

It wasn't until the end of the dive that I realized something had gone horribly wrong and even then, initially, I wasn't certain. As all of the divers returned to the anchor line for the ascent back to the surface, I realized only eleven were present. I looked down and observed Tim holding onto the line, casually looking around for his wife Mary. As I peered out onto the site, I did not see any other movement or bubbles, so I swam down to Tim and signaled the question "where is your buddy?" His response to me, a shrug, caused my stomach to knot. I was certain Mary was not on this site.

There were only a few possible scenarios, only one of which was good. It seemed plausible that Mary had struggled against the current and aborted the dive, but why didn't her buddy and husband know this? My heart raced as I pondered my next course of action. While I preferred to complete my recommended three minute safety stop at fifteen feet, I knew the risk of a direct ascent to the surface was low, so I signaled to my wife that I was going up and for her to buddy up with Tim.

When I reached the surface, the dive master Alex asked if I was okay. I quickly replied "Yes, is Mary onboard?" "No," replied Alex, "Everyone is in the water." I remember responding with "Well then we have a problem, because Mary is not on this site."

Alex asked me if I was certain and I replied that I was. She moved quickly to alert the Captain and other crew members and they began to scan the surface of the water. I waited what seemed like an eternity but was likely only a minute or two before Alex returned. She advised that they spotted something in the water, way off in the distance and thought it might be Mary. The other crew members had jumped into the chase boat and were headed out to see if it was her. Moments later the chase boat crew called in to advise they had located Mary and had her onboard. She was a bit shaken but otherwise okay.

Once everyone was safely on board the boat, we needed some answers. What had gone wrong? How did Mary end up lost at sea and drifting away from the boat without any of the crew noticing her? Why did Tim continue his dive, doing nothing, knowing his wife and buddy had entered the water with him, even though he never saw her during the entire dive? Obviously there was more than one breakdown that needed to be addressed.

Diving is a dangerous activity, even for the most experienced divers. In this case, the combination of low visibility and a moderate current combined with an inattentive crew and lackadaisical husband put Mary in peril. You can add to this Mary's own decision making and failure to use her compass before or during her descent. So what exactly happened?

As Mary and Tim descended, they gave up trying to swim forward into the current, opting instead to drop down to the sand as Michelle and I had done. The only problem was that Tim was far enough forward to still have the anchor line in view and Mary was far enough back that when she hit the sand neither Tim nor the anchor line was in sight. Alone in the sand and with no sense of direction, because she had not taken a compass heading, Mary reported looking around, seeing no one and deciding to abort the dive and return to the boat. This was the best decision she could have made given her situation. Meanwhile, Tim continued on his dive. He reported his reason for continuing to dive was to find his wife. He knew she was experienced and wasn't really worried about her. He wrongly assumed she was somewhere on the site and that if he continued to dive, they would eventually bump into each other and buddy back up. This never occurred.

Mary meanwhile was going through hell. The current was so strong that by the time she surfaced from 60 feet down, she reported being about fifty feet behind the boat. She could see a crew member on deck but the crew member had his back turned to her. She yelled and he didn't hear her. She blew her whistle and he didn't hear her. She tried to swim back to the boat against the current, but quickly tired and gave up. She reported that she wasn't too worried, at least not at first. She followed her training. She inflated her buoyancy compensation device (BCD,) AKA diver's vest) and then her safety sausage (diver below float) and figured any minute someone would turn around and see her. That minute never came.

While Tim continued on his forty minute dive and the crew member sat atop the boat with his back turned, Mary drifted farther and farther away from the boat. As the minutes passed she reported first feeling apprehension, then fear. She had drifted between a half mile and mile from the boat before I realized she was missing, surfaced and notified the crew.

The crew later thanked me for cutting out my safety stop. According to them, a few more minutes made all the difference. Had I not realized she was missing and surfaced when I did, she may have actually disappeared from view, making finding her much more difficult. Many failures occurred on this dive, but in the end we got Mary back, and ultimately that is all that matters. Believe it or not, she was back in the water for the very next dive.

IN THE COMPANY OF DOLPHINS

I often tell my friends that I am okay with dying today, because I have lived more than most humans ever have or ever will. I have had experiences which many only read about in books or see on television and many of these experiences are etched into my very being, they've become part of my soul. Anyone who has had a meaningful interaction with wild dolphins will understand this story.

Cruising aboard the live-aboard dive boat *Juliet*, somewhere between the dive sites of "Space Mountain" and "Hog Heaven" we happened upon a large group of dolphins. The sky was clear blue, there was no wind, just a bright sun, warm on the skin and nearly flat calm seas. As the boat skipped across the water, the joyous jumping of one dolphin, then two, then four finally brought the cry "Dolphins!" The captain slowed the boat to a stop and the crew dropped the ladder into the water. There was no time to waste. Anyone who has attempted to swim with wild dolphins knows how difficult it is to get them to stay. Today was different.

The first to jump in was one of the crew members. I hurried to get my mask, fins and snorkel, passing one fellow diver then another, "getting in," I questioned each one, to the surprising response of "No, they're not going to stay." It did not matter to me, I was getting in.

At first it was just the dive master, me and about a dozen or so dolphins. The dive master told me that we had to keep the dolphins entertained if there was any chance of getting them to stay. So he and I began twirling down, free-diving to the sandy bottom just 45 feet below. Each time I spiraled up or down, one or more of the dolphins would join me, twisting and turning with me, within arm's reach. I remember thinking I was in heaven, was I really dancing with dolphins?

About ten minutes or so into this, one fellow diver after another joined the fray. Then from nowhere came more dolphins and more dolphins. I was now worn out. Diving up and down at a frantic pace, attempting to keep pace with wild dolphins is no easy task. I decided to take a break and just float on the surface. I tried to count the dolphins. At one point I had reached twenty and then I lost count. I later asked one dive master and she said she thought there were maybe thirty or so.

After catching my breath, I again started twirling, staying shallow this time, less than ten feet beneath the surface. Every time I spun myself around a dolphin was spinning with me. It was as if we had become one with the dolphins, two packs, one from land and one from sea, joined together. Everywhere I looked I saw a smiling face. Almost everyone was now in the water, only my wife and the boat's captain remained onboard.

I had lost track of time, the sea had become a bubbling cauldron of dolphins and humans. The encounter can only be called magical. Eventually the captain signaled for us to return to the boat. I was so tired I could barely pull myself up the ladder. Some of my fellow divers struggled to get back to the boat, but all eventually made it safely aboard. I asked the captain how long we had been in the water and I was surprised when he responded forty-five minutes!

The dive master and I had been in the water the entire time. The others had been in anywhere from ten to thirty minutes. One crew member told me that they had never seen anything like it. She said they often encountered the dolphins in this area, but their previous record for interaction was only about fifteen to twenty minutes. We had more than doubled that previous record. While I look forward to another encounter such as this one, I am forced to be realistic. These encounters don't happen every day and certainly not in such beautiful weather conditions, in such calm flat seas, in 45 feet of water, over pure white sand bottoms. This encounter is just one of many reasons, if I died today, I'd die happy.

EL MATADOR

One of the primary reasons for becoming a diver, aside from the fact that my wife strongly encouraged me, was my desire to swim with sharks. From the time I was a young child, I was fascinated with sharks. When I was no more than four, my Father and Uncle Earl would take me shark fishing on the beaches of Florida. As I grew older, I would gather and read every shark book I could find and proudly announce to everyone who would listen - my intention to be an "oceanographer" when I grew up. Not exactly the proper title for one who studies sharks, but I was eight years old, what did I know?

My Aunt Charlotte was known to swim with sharks. I remember standing on the beach watching her swim into the break, where you could see the sharks hanging out just beneath the crests of the waves. I remember her telling me, "Sharks don't eat people sweetie." This was all occurring in the 1970's at a time when there were no personal computers and email was not yet in common use. In fact, telephones didn't even have call waiting and pocket cell phones hadn't been thought of yet. These experiences even pre-dated the movie Jaws. I remember writing letters and drawing pictures of sharks, then mailing them to my Aunt Charlotte. I lived in Maryland and she in Florida, but her and my Uncle Earl were relatives I always looked forward to visiting.

Fast forward now. While I have spent time diving with many different species of sharks (Hammerhead, White Tip, Black Tip, Caribbean Reef, Grey Reef, Nurse, Sand Tiger and Sandbar,) none of them have a reputation as notorious as the Bull Shark. According to Discovery Channel's Shark Week, the Bull Shark is thought to be responsible for most bites on human beings, followed closely by Great

White then Tiger sharks. Bull sharks have been indicated in more U.S. east coast shark attacks than any other species.

It was a beautiful day for diving aboard the *Atlantis IV* out of Atlantic Beach, North Carolina. According to a multiple diving publications, Atlantic Beach, along with Beaufort and Morehead City, North Carolina are considered among the best locations in the world for shipwreck diving. The area is also known for large animal encounters and over the years it has produced surprise visitors ranging from the Whale Shark to the Great White Shark and is home to one of the worlds' largest gatherings of Sand Tiger sharks. The warm clear waters of the gulfstream skirt the North Carolina coast, making for some of the best diving in the world and by far the best diving in the United States.

On this particular day we would be diving on the wreck of the *USS Schurz*, formerly the German vessel *Geier*, a World War I era ship sitting in approximately 115 feet of water on a sandy bottom. My wife and I had been to this site before and it was known to produce nice artifacts. It was and still is the perfect wreck to hunker down in the sand and start digging for treasures.

I looked at my wife and saw that she had found a small section of sand to dig in, not far from the large boilers, which offer the greatest relief on the wreck site. She seemed to be intently working on something so I decided to swim around a little bit and look for my own proverbial pot of gold. Being a good dive buddy meant not straying too far, so after a few minutes I headed back to her position to see what she was doing. I glanced up at the top of the boilers and noticed a couple of our fellow divers swimming somewhat frantically in the direction of the anchor line. Other than being in a hurry, they seemed okay and so no alarms went off in my head. The visibility was 80 feet or more and while we were nearing a required decompression stop on my computer, I had plenty of air remaining to stay a few more minutes.

It was at that moment, as I turned back to look at my wife that I realized why the others were moving a little quicker than usual. There was a solitary shark. Not just any solitary shark, it was a 10 foot Bull shark! He was unmistakable in his presence. He seemed a bit irritated and almost confrontational in his attitude. It appeared he had claimed the boiler area of this shipwreck as his own and we were trespassing.

I tapped my wife on the shoulder and pointed out the shark. To my consternation she continued to work on whatever the heck it was she was working on. I decided to hover above her, watching the sharks' every move. He was not hard to follow, he was circling us. First from a distance, then closer and closer with each passing loop. I knew from my studies of sharks that many species will make close passes, then eventually bump an intended target before moving on to the final stage – an attack!

The Bull shark continued circling us, I looked at my dive computer and it was showing a required four minute decompression stop at ten feet. I tapped my wife one last time and made a strongly suggestive motion that it was time to go. She made one last tug on the item she had been digging up and it came loose into her grasp. She looked at it, shrugged and put it in her goodie bag. The Bull shark's last circle was just a few feet away and as he passed by I made a suggestive wave like a matador fighting a bull. As we swam away toward the anchor line I feared he would follow, but he did not. I kept glancing back at the amazing predator I had just encountered and wondered just how close I had come to being taste tested. The shark simply widened his circular passes around the boilers, back to his original range. I could see him below as I ascended the line. This is another of those images that is seared into my brain.

As we stepped back onto the swim platform of the boat, the dive master Renate greeted us with a huge smile and a question "Didn't you guys see the bull shark?" "Did we see him?", I replied, "We had a bullfight!" Unknown to me and my Michelle, our dive group had abandoned us when they saw the shark. I had happened to see the last two of them racing to the anchor line. Without really thinking about it, we had just faced down a rogue, solitary bull shark who was being very territorial about his ship wreck. We didn't do it on purpose, and with afterthought our slow response may have placed us in grave danger, but we lived to tell the tale.

While I have total respect for all sharks and especially the top five most dangerous (Bull, Great White, Tiger, Oceanic White Tip and Mako,) I felt a serene sense about this bull shark. I was aware of his presence and I made eye contact with him as he circled, but I never felt threatened or in danger. I remember feeling a mutual curiosity between the shark and I, each of us sizing up the other and almost playfully deciding to move on. This was a truly amazing encounter.

SEALED WITH A KISS

More than one story in this book comes from my experience aboard the *Solmar V* live-aboard boat out of Cabo San Lucas, Mexico. The *Solmar V* travels a variety of itineraries (Socorro Islands, Isle de Guadalupe and the Sea of Cortez.) On this trip Michelle and I would be diving in the Sea of Cortez. While most of our trips are done with a small group of friends, this particular trip we were going it alone.

Upon arriving in Cabo San Lucas, we boarded the boat. At first I thought I was in the wrong place. As I looked around, I saw a number of senior citizens onboard and I thought I was boarding a sight-seeing boat filled with old people for a shoreline evening cruise. I was in fact on the right boat, but I quickly learned our dive buddies for the week were two groups of seniors, one from Detroit, Michigan and another from San Diego, California. I remember thinking to myself, "This ought to be a trip."

We discovered that these two groups of seniors were all divers between the ages of 65 and 84. The week-long trip turned out to be one of my all-time favorites, partly due to the diving and partly due to the company of my new found friends. Not only were they seniors, they were excellent divers and not afraid to get wet.

The Sea of Cortez is a diving treasure unto itself. It is filled with marine life and a portion of the Cabo Pulma National Marine Sanctuary is housed by the sea. One of the highlights of this trip was to be searching for Whale sharks and having the chance to snorkel with these mammoth creatures. Unfortunately we could not find them, even with the ultra-light plane put up to search for them. It didn't matter to Michelle and I, a different attraction provided more than ample entertainment.

Large colonies of seals and sea lions joined us on many of the dives. These playful creatures seemed to be checking us out as much as we were checking them out. Diving with us on both our daytime and nighttime dives, they playfully interacted with us, swimming circles around us, jetting between our legs and gliding over our shoulders.

I spent a good deal of time video-taping this adventure and one interaction joins many of my other special underwater moments, the ones that tell me my life has been a good one. In clear shallow water with the sun beams shining through, I noticed a nearly pure-white sea lion, a completely different color than the rest. It was an albino for lack of a better term. It began to follow my wife and I and we noticed that it had been injured, one of its eyes was scarred and closed shut, leaving it only one eye from which to see. To this day I'm not sure if it was a male or female, it doesn't matter, it was a beautiful and curious creature.

I moved a slight distance away from Michelle in an attempt to get a nice wide angle shot of her and the sea lion swimming together in my video. Just moments later the sea lion moved in very close to my wife and as she turned to look at the sea lion, it stretched out its neck and came nose to nose with my wife in a moment of pure bliss, a moment frozen in time. It was an Eskimo kiss that neither my wife nor I will ever forget. While I didn't get the best angle on my video clip, it was the most amazing thing to see in person.

This creature seemed to long for our attention and the touch of a human being. This was a magical moment and yet another blessing in my life.

Sea lion kissing Michelle (Photo by Ken Barrick)

STEVE'S BOMMIE

Australia, the Great Barrier Reef and the Coral Sea; now that I have your attention, the Coral Sea and more specifically a dive site named Steve's Bommie are where our Outback adventure begins. In Australian, bommie is the word used to describe a sea mount or pinnacle jetting up from the ocean floor. In the Coral Sea, pinnacles can be massive ecosystems unto themselves, full of undersea life.

Our trip to Australia was an amazing journey and included several days in the outback with the Aborigines, white water rafting on the Tully River, an amazing riverboat journey down the Daintree River, a tour of Port Douglas, a stay in Cairns and our five day excursion aboard the *Journey*, our dive boat extraordinaire.

I came home from this trip with many stories to tell, but two of them occurred on one dive site and both are etched into my mind forever. The first involves our approach to Steve's Bommie. As the *Journey* approached the anchor site, the cry of "whale" came loud and clear from one of the crew. The boat sputtered to a halt and the Captain advised that anyone wishing to snorkel with the whales should grab their mask fins and snorkel quickly, as the whales usually don't stay long. It was imperative to jump in the water now.

The first person in the water was one of the crew members and I was a quick second. I looked back and no one else was getting in. It was just the two of us. I remember the first time I put my face in the water; it's as clear to me today as it was in that moment. I looked down and beneath me several feet away was this massive moving creature. It was a slow moving blur of black and white and at first I thought it was an Orca, but I was wrong. As it slipped from my view, I looked up for the crew member, whose name I didn't know and asked him what it was. "Minke Whale" he exclaimed!

He told me to stay motionless on the surface. If we chased the whales, he advised, we would scare them away. If we stayed put, they would come back to check us out. I looked back at the boat and still none of the other divers had bothered to get in and the boat seemed to be drifting farther and farther away. I waited, fearing that one brief moment was all I would experience, but my fear would soon turn to joy.

Lying motionless on the surface of the Coral Sea, with the nearest land a hundred miles away and the boat seemingly drifting over the horizon, I suddenly felt vulnerable. For the first time in my diving career, I realized it was just me, one crew member and the sea's creatures. While the feeling was a bit scary, it was also awe inspiring and brought me the sense that I was a true adventurer. This moment is yet another I think of when I tell people, I do not fear death, for I have lived.

As that thought subsided I felt the water move beneath me. I looked down and to my amazement I saw two Minke whales, a very large one and a much smaller one, a juvenile with a parent! The dive master yelled to me it was a full pod, he had counted a total of five whales! Instinctively I dove down to swim beside them as they went by and I gazed into the adult's eye. I don't know what the whale was thinking, but I was mentally numb. I was in such awe of what I was seeing and what I was doing that I literally could have died and went to heaven in that moment.

The whales stayed with us for just another pass before becoming bored with us and moving on, but the moment was worth one million moments on land and one I will forever cherish. The Captain was now signaling for the two of us to re-board the *Journey* and had moved the boat back into position to pick us up.

Once back on board I discovered why none of the other crew or my fellow divers had entered the water. The crew knew the story and one of them had shared it with the other divers, which gave them pause in jumping in. The story of why the dive site was named Steve's Bommie.

Apparently just a few years earlier, another dive boat had been visiting the pinnacle and observed a pod of Minke whales. The dive master on the boat, a fellow named Steve decided to jump in and swim with the whales. Steve disappeared and was never heard from again.

The belief and the story told around the port town was that Steve had likely gotten too close to one of the whales and was struck by a fin or a tale, subsequently knocking him unconscious and causing him to drown. Steve's body was never recovered.

I don't know what I would have done if I had heard the story before I jumped in, but I know this; If I would have died in that moment, I would have died a happy man and I'm quite certain, Steve felt the same way. RIP Steve.

The second story about Steve's Bommie is a reminder that anything can happen at any time while SCUBA diving. It was a gorgeous sunny day and I had already completed a couple of wonderful dives. I had made the decision to sit the next dive out, opting to do a little sunbathing on the top deck of the *Journey*. I was the only member of our group taking a break, as Michelle joined with another member of our group for the dive.

I had just closed my eyes and begun to feel the warmth of the pacific sun when I heard the first cry for help. I was not certain what I heard the first time, but the second cry came through loud and clear, "Help, Bernie needs help!"

Bernie and his wife Carol were excellent divers. Bernie was also a large man, a former NHL Hockey player. I'd estimate he was every bit of 6'4" and 280 solid pounds.

I jumped to my feet and peered out from the top aft deck of the boat. I could not see anyone, but I could hear the repeated yells, "Help, Bernie needs help!" I looked down and saw the dive master standing on the swim platform, frozen as if in a mental panic, locked in position. I looked around and saw no one else. I could not see Carol or Bernie, but I had to assume they were hidden behind the chase boat which floated approximately twenty or thirty yards behind the *Journey*.

I ran down the stairs and without much forethought, passed the panic stricken dive master and dove head first into the open ocean, no mask, no fins, no snorkel and swam toward the chase boat. As I turned the corner, I saw Carol struggling to keep Bernie's head above water. She too was panicked, but at least had the presence of mind to hold onto him. Bernie was motionless.

I swam around and inflated his BCD, something Carol had not thought to do in the urgency of the situation. I told her to let him go and I began to pull him back to the *Journey*. He was awake and breathing but unresponsive. The awake and breathing parts gave me some sense of relief and the unresponsiveness in combination gave me a preliminary diagnosis. I had seen this before during an open water training class, Bernie was having a panic attack.

Struggling to pull a 6'4," 280lb hockey player in full dive gear twenty or thirty yards in the open ocean with no fins, in three to four foot seas is no easy task. I have no trouble admitting I was struggling to get it done. I yelled to the dive master who was still on the swim platform to come and help. This seemed to snap her from her stupor. She removed her shirt and dove in. She met me about half way and together we pulled Bernie back to the swim platform, removed his dive gear and hoisted him onto the deck. All this time, he was unresponsive, gazing up at the sky.

Another crew member arrived and we lifted Bernie into a seated position and finally he responded. Our question was simple, "Bernie are you OK?", to which he replied "What happened?" I went through a series of questions with him. He knew his name, his wife, where he was, how old he was etc... and it appeared he was coming out of it. While the dive master reviewed his computer for any safety violations, I began questioning Carol as to what had happened.

She told us they were doing a normal controlled descent down to the top of the pinnacle, which was about 60 feet beneath the surface. She said on the way down, at about thirty or forty feet, Bernie began flailing his arms around and kicking frantically for the surface. He had kept his regulator in his mouth the entire time. She followed him to the surface not knowing what was wrong. When she arrived at the surface she found him struggling to keep his head above water and he would not respond to her. She grabbed him and held his head above water and began yelling for help. Luckily they had ascended very close to the chase boat and she was able to hold onto the chase boat with one hand and hold onto him with the other until I had arrived.

Carol was not a rescue diver, so she did not have the knowledge or skill based training to act properly in the situation. If she had this training, she most certainly would have thought to inflate his BCD, release his weights and begin towing him back to the boat. It was a mere stroke of luck that the situation had such a positive outcome.

In the end it was decided that Bernie had succumbed to spatial disorientation leading to a panic attack. He later noted that he had started to feel "weird" during his descent and with the top of the pinnacle so far beneath him, he started to succumb to the sensation of vertigo. He felt wobbly and began anxious which quickly built to a full blown panic attack. In full panic mode, Bernie had but one thought, to get to the surface. He did in fact reach the surface but made no effort to inflate his own BCD or ditch his weights. He struggled against himself to keep his head above water. Lucky for him, his wife Carol was with him, and while she didn't take all the appropriate actions, she did enough to keep him alive until help arrived.

Once all the divers returned to the boat, we pulled up anchor from Steve's Bommie and bid it farewell. I had experienced magic with the whales and had participated in saving a life. I remember sleeping very well that evening. I was at peace with the world.

SEX CHANGE

One of the more humorous, but not so humorous stories I have to share happened in a local diving spot in Delta Pennsylvania. Guppy Gulch quarry has been used for many years as a training quarry. It is approximately a one hour drive from downtown Baltimore, Maryland.

I owned a dive shop, Off the Wall Scuba for three years, from 2007 to 2010. In that time we trained many new divers and we would also receive calls from certified divers looking for someone to spend a day or weekend diving. In most cases one of my staff would accommodate these requests, however if we didn't have any staff available, we would match them up with local divers we knew made good buddies. In many cases we would put a newer or returning diver with a much more experienced diver, putting them at ease and giving them an opportunity to pick an experienced divers brain. We knew who our experienced divers were and which ones enjoyed working with divers both new and returning to the sport after a long hiatus.

In this particular case, myself and a couple experienced divers had planned to spend a relaxing day diving at Guppy Gulch. One of my fellow divers had purchased some new diving equipment and was planning to test it out. Not long before heading out the door for the drive to Guppy Gulch, I received a phone call from a gentleman looking to do some diving. He advised me that he was a certified diver, but it had been many years since he had been in the water. He was looking for someone to dive with.

I told him, it's short notice, but if you'd like to join me, I'm heading out to do some diving this morning. He was excited! He told me he would meet us at the quarry in an hour.

My fellow divers and I checked in at the front desk and began setting up our dive gear. I looked around for any sign of our new friend but could not locate him. We waited fifteen minutes and then I called his cell phone. He did not answer. We decided to move on and start our diving day.

We walked down to the water where we observed an older, overweight gentleman gearing up in what could most nicely be described as vintage SCUBA gear. "Are you Ron?" I asked. He looked up with a big smile and in a serious country drawl blurted out "You must be Ken!"

My fellow divers and I politely smiled and discreetly gave each other the "you've got to be kidding" look, but Ron was ready to dive.

Our plan was quite simple; there were five of us diving in our group. We were going to visit the *Damn Phool*, a pleasure boat purposely sunk in 55 feet of water. It was one of the primary attractions in Guppy Gulch quarry. It was not the easiest of diving. The water temperatures on the Damn Phool were forty-five degrees Fahrenheit year round. While the visibility could be thirty feet on a good day, typical visibility ranged from just inches to several feet. The more students training in the quarry, the worse the visibility gets. Today, it looked like we were going to get lucky, there were no dive shops conducting student training and we only noticed one other couple entering the water, a wife and husband dive team.

The plan was for me to lead and the other four to follow, staying in two man buddy teams, side by side behind me. We all descended together and started our dive on a submerged training platform 18 feet below. The quarry has many training platforms, all of them connected by a line system so that it is easy to navigate from one platform to another and then from the final platform out to the different submerged attractions. I had been diving in this quarry many times and I knew the rope system and where each led like the back of my hand.

We left the first platform and followed the line to the second platform. Upon arriving at the second platform I noticed a severe drop in the visibility, from about ten feet to less than two. I bumped into the husband and wife couple, who I assumed were mucking up the visibility by practicing some skills near the bottom. My goal was to get away from that mess as quickly as possible. I looked back and counted my four divers. They were all now on the platform. I motioned that we were continuing on.

Typically when I lead a group of divers, depending on their experience level, I will swim about ten kick cycles and then look back to make sure they are all still with me. Usually however I am leading student divers and in those cases, I will actually take up a position off to the side of the group so that I can maintain visual contact with them the entire time. Today I had a group of experienced divers so I decided to lead from the front.

When I looked back after my first ten kick cycles I counted only three divers behind me. Where was number four? I immediately noticed the missing diver was our new friend Ron. One by one I signaled my fellow divers asking each of them where Ron was and one by one they all shrugged. How, I thought , can three of my experienced dive buddies all misplace one diver?

I motioned to them that I was ascending to the surface to look for Ron's bubbles and for them to continue their dive. They had all been to Guppy Gulch before and knew where they were going. I ascended to the surface and looked out over the entire area. I remember thinking to myself - he couldn't have gone far, he didn't know the quarry and he certainly didn't appear as though he'd be a fast mover. I scanned the surface and saw no bubbles except those from my group. A horrible feeling came over me; there were no bubbles because Ron had drowned.

I quickly swam back to shore hoping to find Ron, hoping that he had aborted the dive and would be sitting on shore shaking his head because he had some equipment issue or just didn't feel right. I arrived on shore and could not locate Ron. I ran back down to the water and could not see bubbles anywhere. I ran to the office and asked if anyone had left through the front gate; no one had.

I informed the quarry staff of my fears. My heart had sunk into my stomach. I advised the staff that I was re-entering the water to conduct a search of the area where I had last seen Ron. The staff was going to launch a kayak to search the outer parts of the quarry, out of view from our position on the shore, for surface bubbles or any other signs of a diver.

As I swam alone along the bottom of the quarry, checking under each platform, my anxiety level built, expecting that I would come across the lifeless body of a fellow diver. I searched the entire shallow part of the quarry and did not find Ron. None of this was adding up.

I surfaced and found one of my fellow dive buddies John on the surface. He too had been searching for Ron and found nothing. The other two from our group were now returning to shore and we all gathered together wondering what could possibly have happened to Ron. Where could he be?

The quarry staff member returned to dock and reported seeing some bubbles out around the corner, in a deeper area. He could not be certain how many divers were below, but he said there was definitely more than one. We convinced ourselves that it was the husband and wife couple we had run into on the platform earlier. We pondered our next move in locating Ron. Was it time to call the authorities?

As we stood on the dock discussing our next search efforts, the bubbles appeared from around the corner and slowly made their way back to shore. A few moments later, one head popped up then another, then a third... it was Ron! I took a big deep breath. Thank God!

I didn't know whether to hug Ron or give him a swift kick in the pants. How did he end up with the husband and wife couple? As Ron and the couple exited the water, we just had to know. I remember looking at the attractive, well figured woman and then at Ron. "Ron?" I asked, "Can't you tell the difference between a man and a woman? You got into the water with four men and you exit the water with a woman."

Ron smiled at me and in that deep southern drawl said "Look at her, do you blame me?" I went on to explain to him everything that was happening while he was off ogling some woman's cute little booty. He explained that he didn't do it on purpose. Apparently when we ran across the couple on that second swim platform, given that the visibility was so bad, he had inadvertently thought they were part of our group. He didn't realize it was a man and a woman until much later into the dive when the visibility improved. At that point it was too late and so he decided he was safer to stay with them than he was to come looking for us. I'm very glad Ron was OK, but I could have killed him.

The lesson here is to know who you're diving with and take a good hard look at the gear they are wearing and what they look like when you first enter the water. This might eliminate confusion in low visibility situations.

LEAP OF FAITH II

The diving community was ecstatic a few years back when a movie featuring the sport hit the big screen. It was titled "Open Water" and was based on a story about a young couple who became lost at sea while SCUBA diving in the Bahamas. The movie was bad, but the story behind it was even more tragic, as the young couple it was based on had in fact disappeared and never been heard from again. The movie writers took the story of their disappearance and assigned the couple a fictional ending. While the ending was one of many possible demises the couple may have met, it seemed a bit far-fetched.

To save you the trouble of rescuing this movie from the Walmart™ bargain bin, I'll share the ending with you. The primary male character (the husband) is eaten by sharks, and his wife, presumably out of fear of being eaten alive, decides to remove her buoyancy control device and commit suicide by drowning herself. In one of the last scenes before the couple succumbs to the sharks; they are seen looking down, watching the sharks circle beneath them.

With this as a backdrop, having just seen the movie in our local theater, my wife and I headed off to Australia and five days of diving the Coral Sea and Great Barrier Reef. The Coral Sea is real "Open Water." If my memory serves me correctly, it was approximately a seventeen hour crossing by boat from Cairns to our final destination.

While I have many great memories from my visit to the outback, and more than one of them have made it into this book, this is one of my favorites. We had just completed one of our dives and everyone was back on board the boat. The captain asked our group if we had seen any sharks below. Not a single diver, including me, the one many call the "shark man" because I'm always spotting sharks, had observed one.

The captain insisted the sharks were present on the dive site but very skittish. "Yeah, Yeah" I said, laughing him off, "there are no sharks on this dive site."

The captain disappeared for a few minutes and then returned with a couple juicy steaks. I was hungry and thought great, he's firing up the grill. I went about my business rinsing down my gear and slipping out of my wetsuit. A few moments later I heard a loud commotion at the back of the boat. I went to investigate. There was the captain, dangling a five or six foot shark above the swim platform; so much for my steak dinner.

The shark had latched onto a piece of steak and was intent on taking it back into the water with him. As the shark flailed around and my fellow divers gathered, a large number of sharks began appearing at the back of the boat. The captain banged the shark a few times against the side of the boat and finally the little fellow let go. The captain then lowered the steak back into the water and a mad dash ensued, with four or five sharks fighting to get a hold of that treasured snack.

As the captain once again brought the rope from the water, two sharks had a hold of it. The combined weight of the sharks would not allow a full lift from the water, so he pulled them onto the swim platform and they slithered around like two snakes fighting over a mouse. One let go of the steak and nearly grabbed the captain by the leg. He just barely side-stepped that mouth in time and gave the shark a swift kick in the ass, pushing it back into the water. He played with these sharks until all three pieces of steak had been lost to the sharks.

When the captain was done playing he walked over to me and with his strong Aussie accent said "No sharks in the water eh mate?" "That was quite a show" I said, "How do we get to see them in the water?" "Just wait" he said, walking away with a devilish Aussie grin on his face.

We were done diving for the day, but there was a night dive ahead. I went off to take my usual in-between diving and dinner nap. Not long after dozing off I heard the dinner announcement and headed to meet the group for a nice sit down meal. We talked about our day of diving and discussed our plan for the night dive. In the time between my afternoon dive, my nap and dinner, I had pretty much forgotten about the sharks. Yes, I knew they were there but I also knew they were afraid of us. They hadn't come anywhere near us during our day dives.

I love night diving. There is nothing like it. Some of the coolest sea creatures come out of hiding when it's dark. Octopus and squid, lobster and tiger tails, all come out and their colors pop on night dives when you use proper lighting.

As with most night dives, our plan was to dive on the same site as our afternoon dive; this would lessen our chance of getting lost. I didn't give any thought to the sharks being there. I donned my gear and decided I would be first in the water. I was anxious to get below.

Left foot first, I took my giant stride off the swim platform, splashing into the darkness below. This was a true night dive, not a twilight dive. It was pitch black, no moon, only the glowing lights of the dive boat to find my way back. For many, night diving itself is a major leap of faith, but in most cases, it is easier to do than daytime diving. In other words, at night, it is not hard to find a bright or flashing light (attached to the boat,) in the middle of the ocean, no matter how far you travel from it.

I hit the water and floated on the surface awaiting the rest of the group. Michelle was just stepping onto the swim platform when I decided to shine my light into the darkness below. I was looking to see if anything interesting was swimming beneath me. I did a double take and then a triple take. There were at least a dozen sharks swimming in a large slow moving circle not more than ten feet beneath me. I looked up at Michelle and a couple of others in line who were waiting to do their entries; "It looks like Open Water (the movie) in here" I said. "What do you mean?" Michelle asked curiously. I calmly informed her that there were a dozen or more sharks circling me as I spoke.

"Yeah right" was the response from a few of my fellow divers. "Alright, come on in" I invited. I figured the more people in the water, the less chance of me being the one eaten. The captain leaned over the side and said "I told you to just wait eh mate," to which my fellow divers replied in unison, "Is he serious, are the sharks there?" The captain and I both refused to answer. "Come on in, the waters' fine" I said… and with that I ducked my head beneath the surface and began my dive.

As I descended through the center of the shark circle they moved from my path. Once I had broken through the barrier I did not see them for the rest of the dive. This was another leap of faith. While I had spent significant hours in the water with many species of sharks, I had never before been circled by so many while I was on the surface and I had never descended through such a circle of razor sharp teeth on a night dive. It was un-nerving to know they were there, always just out of reach of my dive light, not knowing if they were behind me or beneath me. It didn't help that I had just watched the movie Open Water, but one more time, I took that leap of faith… and lived to tell about it.

Ken Barrick

RE-LIVING OPERATION HAILSTORM

During a holiday party at our local dive shop, Michelle and I were mingling with the guests when the topic of an upcoming dive trip to Truk Lagoon came up. We overheard our friends Harry and Julie, whom we had met on previous trips, asking the shop owner Charles as to whether or not all the spots were filled and whether or not the trip was going to take place. Charles replied that two spots remained open and that this may cause the trip to be canceled.

Michelle and I had just returned from Australia a few months earlier and the prospect of another expensive trip, this one to Truk Lagoon in Micronesia, hadn't been a consideration for us. We glanced at each other, each thinking the same thought, could we afford a seven-thousand dollar dive trip? The answer was truly no.

As the party continued and we drank more "cheer," I jokingly told Harry that Michelle and I were considering going to Truk. It was one of the biggest and best mistakes I have ever made. The rest of the party Harry and Julie made comments to us about going and the more we drank, the looser my wallet became. After another hour or so of drinking I asked Michelle what she thought about going to Truk and she muttered one of my favorite phrases, "What the hell, you only live once!" I walked over to Charles and plunked the credit card on the counter, "We'll take those last two spots to Truk!"

I am not a war historian, but one of my favorite pieces of history to share with anyone who will listen is the story of "Operation Hailstorm." I did not know the story before my visit to Truk, but after visually re-living the battle that took place there, I came home with images in my mind that I will never forget.

Truk Lagoon, officially known as Chuuck and located within the Federated States of Micronesia is an enclosed body of water in the middle of the Pacific Ocean. In World War II it was the staging ground for the Japanese Pacific Fleet. The ships and planes that attacked Pearl Harbor launched from this tiny island nation. The lagoon itself is protected by many island mountains and today is a safe harbor for ships crossing the Pacific Ocean. In World War II it was occupied and controlled by Japan.

After the Japanese bombed Pearl Harbor, the U.S. made plans to retaliate and Operation Hailstorm was planned. When the U.S. made its bombing run on the Japanese fleet at Truk Lagoon, sixty four Japanese ships were summarily sunk. An overwhelming number of them were transport ships, known as Maru or merchant ships and they carried everything from Zero fighter planes to tanks, military vehicles and spare parts. One ship was a destroyer named the *Fumizuki*.

There are only three places on earth considered exceptional for historical wreck diving, North Carolina, Truk Lagoon - sometimes referred to as "The Graveyard of the Pacific," and Scapa Flow off the coast of Scotland, where the German fleet was scuttled near the end of World War I.

I had often made the trip to North Carolina, but this was my first wreck diving visit to Truk. I would be diving on yet another live-aboard dive vessel, the *Truk Aggressor*. The journey to Truk Lagoon is a long one from Baltimore, Maryland. We flew from Baltimore to Houston, Texas, Houston to Honolulu, Hawaii, Honolulu to Guam and Guam to Weno, one of the main islands in Micronesia to board the *Truk Aggressor*. We even had to take a dinghy ride from the dock to board the boat because the water was too shallow for the one-hundred plus foot long vessel.

There is no one story to tell you about this journey, rather it is the collection of moments I shall try to describe. I remember the first time I began a descent. The water was a beautiful shade of blue and the sunbeams danced beneath the surface illuminating the shiny fish below. I don't even recall the name of the wreck we were descending on, but I recall the imagery.

I looked down and beneath me was this massive ship, sitting upright with just a bit of a lean. On the forward deck was a tank, a world war two era Japanese tank. I remember thinking to myself "You've got to be kidding me." I looked out toward Michelle who was hovering just off the deck adjacent to the tank and she was pointing at something. I swam closer and observed my very first Lionfish. It was huge and beautiful and flaring it's poisonous tips warning me not to come any closer. I looked back at the tank and noticed what appeared to be a gas mask and then I noticed spent shell casings. I looked back up and noticed a deck gun pointing up, as if still in action, firing at the American bombers. I could visualize the Japanese sailor manning the deck gun and the chaos of the attack.

In North Carolina the wrecks have been decimated by years of "picking" by divers. The difference between North Carolina and Truk Lagoon is that all of the artifacts remain in place on the Truk Lagoon wrecks. There is a large sign at the dock which states: Removal of artifacts will result in a $10,000.00 fine. The people of Truk Lagoon take this very seriously. Being caught with just one spent shell casing will result in the fine, no if's ands or buts. Baggage checks at the airport are extremely thorough when you leave. I suspect airport security personnel who find artifacts in departing guests' baggage are touted as heroes. Ten thousand dollars is a small fortune to the people of Truk Lagoon. The fact that the wrecks and their artifacts are so well protected makes diving in Truk Lagoon worth the journey. Everything is still there, the way it went down nearly seventy years ago.

As I dropped down into a cargo hold I recognized the fuselage and set about searching for the markings to confirm my find. Yes, it was a zero fighter plane!

On another wreck I swam into an interior room the *Truk Aggressor* crew had told me about and discovered human bones. The "operating room" as it was called where injured sailors were taken by doctors during the assault. It is an absolutely amazing place to reflect on just what you are seeing. Many Japanese sailors went down with their ships and their bodies were never recovered. This is truly a graveyard.

Throughout the week, dive after dive brought visual imagery you cannot and will not forget. From torpedo's to periscopes, fighter planes to tanks, human skulls and bones, deck guns and shell casings to amazing life, including Lionfish, Giant Clams, Spotted Eagle Rays, Black-tip Sharks and so much more, Truk Lagoon is a "must dive" destination.

My favorite story from this trip is due to the pure insanity of it. For the entire week of dives our air supply consisted of single aluminum 80 SCUBA tanks. We had no backup pony bottles or spare airs, just a single tank and a dive buddy with the same.

On one particular dive, we were briefed that we'd be doing a true penetration dive. There would be one way in and one way out of the wreck. We would need our dive lights and we would need to follow the plan in order for everyone to make it back out safely, and oh, by the way, the dive would exceed the recreational depth limit of 130 feet.

I wondered to myself if this was a good idea, but no one else in our group seemed too concerned. We were all excellent divers and we had not had any problems with any of the limited penetration dives on the trip. I put on my gear and plunged in with the group.

Checking my depth gauge, it read 130 feet as I approached the stairwell leading down into the interior cargo hold. I knew that as soon as I started down that ladder, I was beyond recreational limits. The dive master had told us we might reach 150 feet on this dive. The plan seemed simple enough. Descend down the staircase and turn right. By going right and keeping the wall on our right, we would tour the four outer walls of the expansive room and end up back at the staircase to exit up and out. While making our way around the room, looking to our left, we would see a large cache of 1930's and 1940's automobiles which had went down with the ship. This seemed simple enough.

The dive master made his way down the staircase followed closely by Julie, then Harry, then me, then Michelle. One by one we followed each other around the wall. The key to making this a safe and pleasant dive was maintaining good buoyancy control. If anyone went too high or too low, then sediment would be disturbed and visibility could quickly go to zero, making for an extremely hazardous condition known as "silt out."

As I turned the first corner I was greeted by a wall of dust. My light went dark; I could no longer see its' beam. I was in total darkness. I stopped and thought for a second. I was fighting to maintain my composure and not let anxiety get the best of me. I remembered being told in the dive briefing not to leave the wall under any circumstances. He said it was too easy to get lost in the middle and not find your way out. I thought for a second and decided to leave the wall.

I motioned for Michelle to go around me. I wanted her to stay on the wall and I hoped that she was doing okay. I motioned for her to go ahead and I proceeded out into the middle of the automobiles. As I let go of the wall and swam into the middle, perhaps by pure stroke of luck, I emerged from the "silt out" into a clear expanse of rows of automobiles. From my new position I could see the lights of my fellow divers marching in line along the wall and one of the funniest, yet most dangerous things I've ever witnessed underwater, Harry's fins puffing up the sediment behind him, leaving everyone else to fight through the clouds of dust. I visualized Pig Pen dragging his blanket in the Peanuts© cartoons. I laughed and my mask began to flood.

I swam across the automobiles and rejoined my wife and fellow divers at the stairwell. I was perhaps the only person, besides Julie and Harry, who enjoyed the dive. Michelle gave me hell for sending her ahead of me and placing her in line behind Harry. I still hear about that decision to this very day.

While everything turned out just fine and I captured some very cool video of the automobiles, I still question my own intelligence for agreeing to a 150 foot completely enclosed penetration dive using only a single aluminum 80 tank. I don't recommend this type of activity as it is beyond the scope of recreational dive training.

Truk lagoon will fill your mind with memories. Whether you are just starting out or you're an experienced technical diver, there is something there for you. You can do land based diving or dive from one of the live-aboard vessels, either way, you will re-live the amazing experience of "Operation Hailstorm." I personally guarantee it.

PROTEUS 8-17-2010

There are not enough adjectives to describe the experience I had with five fellow divers on August 17, 2010. Let me preface this story by telling you what I wrote in my log book that day - "number one dive of all time – anywhere, my adrenaline was pumping – possibly 40 – 50 sharks or more."

You have to know me to understand the enormity of that statement," number one dive of all time." You see, by 2010 I had been diving for more than thirteen years, amassing more than two thousand dives. I had been to some of the world's top diving destinations: the Great Barrier Reef in Australia, Truk Lagoon in Micronesia, Bonaire, Curacao, Utila, Roatan, the Sea of Cortez, the islands of the Bahamas, the Caymans etc... and here I was claiming the very best dive of all time just happened in North Carolina, USA.

Diving from the vessel *Atlantis IV* out of Atlantic Beach North Carolina, something I had done almost annually since 1998, I already knew a good day lay ahead. Let's face it, there was a reason I had visited the area almost annually for more than a decade. The diving was always good. In fact, sometimes it was great and on many occasions when asked about my favorite place to dive, North Carolina always rolled off my tongue, but not like this. Today was better.

On this trip I had brought along a SCUBA instructor friend named Mel and his student Tom, neither of whom had been diving off the Carolina coast. Also along for the trip were my friends Dave and Sue and my wife Michelle. For years I had billed this trip as being "the" best place to dive on earth and it took some convincing to get Mel to come along. He just refused to believe the best diving on earth was a short drive down the eastern seaboard.

I had never visited the wreck of the *Proteus.* My history in North Carolina had taken me to see many great dive sites, the *U-352,* the *USS Shurz* (formerly the German boat Geier,) the *Spar,* the *Askabad,* the *Endra,* the *Bedfordshire, Aeolus, Naeco,* and others, but this week we were pushing into new territory, spending one full day farther north visiting the *Proteus* and *Caribsea.*

Our group had already completed a couple of great dives and was looking forward to what the new day would bring. We boarded the *Atlantis IV* and pushed off from the dock just before 7:00am. By 10:18am we were splashing into the Atlantic Ocean to begin our 120 ft descent to the wreck below. On the way down the anchor line I remember feeling blah. The visibility didn't seem very good and upon arriving on the wreck, I remember thinking there wasn't much in the way of fish life. In a flash, things changed.

Wreck of the Proteus (Photo by Ken Barrick)

Michelle and I separated from the group and headed off toward the bow; following the ships contour I saw one shark, then two, then I lost count. They were everywhere. The visibility opened up as the sun broke through the clouds and the water began to sparkle some 120 feet beneath the surface. Suddenly there were sharks above us, below us, in front and behind. Sharks were swimming over my left shoulder and between my legs. I looked ahead and saw Michelle snapping pictures with her camera. I felt something swipe the side of my head and turned to see a massive body going by. The shark's pectoral fin had brushed my left ear.

Wreck of the Proteus (Photo by Ken Barrick)

All through this dive I had my video camera rolling. This dive produced some of the best shark footage I have ever shot. I looked back at Michelle and she seemed to be scampering, if one can scamper underwater, toward me. I have one shot where she is surrounded by seven sharks in the frame. This is the dive where I met my sand tiger shark buddy I named Fuzzy. Fuzzy was a juvenile sand tiger shark, about five or six feet long with who knows what stuck in his teeth. He followed me everywhere. Every time I turned around Fuzzy was nipping, not quite literally, at my fins.

Ken with sand tiger shark (Photo by Michelle Barrick)

After spending several minutes in "shark city," Michelle and I headed back to the anchor line to begin our ascent to the boat. For my fellow divers reading this, you will understand, but for the rest of you, it is highly unusual for sharks to follow divers back to the boat. In fact, in my thirteen years of diving, I had never before observed sharks doing safety stops with divers. In North Carolina and I'm sure in many other places around the world, it is not unusual to have barracuda hanging out with you during safety stops, but not sharks.

As we ascended the water became bluer and almost for as far as the eye could see, there were sharks. At 100 feet, then 80, then 60 and all the way to the 20 foot mark, the sharks were with us, swimming just a few feet away. They were above and below. My adrenaline was still pumping, taking in the amazing experience we were having. I used my video camera to capture a large seven footer swimming between Sue's legs then two more heading straight toward Michelle in a slow, methodical and curious way. Mel was below me rolling his own video, trying to capture "moments" to share with our land-loving friends.

One large shark came in so close I decided to start counting his teeth, he hovered just an arm's length away as if he was patiently waiting for me to pet him. My heart pounded loudly all the way up the ladder and was still pounding like a tax collector at the door when I sat down to remove my gear. I stood up in time to see Mel stepping onto the boat. I looked at him and he had this stupid, silly grin on his face. "So what did you think of that one?" I asked. His reply, "That was awesome." He went on to tell me that his adrenaline was still pumping. "Join the club" I told him.

He asked me if this is what North Carolina diving was like all the time. "Yep" I replied, "Now do you understand why I wanted you to come?" It just doesn't get any better than North Carolina, USA and on this day, I rest my case.

HARBOR SHARK

There are not many exciting stories to tell you about my commercial diving business in Baltimore Maryland. There are good stories, but not many exciting ones. This story is an exception to that rule.

A typical work day for me and my staff is the mundane job of cleaning boat hulls in the Baltimore Harbor. Since 2002, my company KB Diver Services has grown into the most active underwater services company in the Mid-Atlantic region. In a typical season we will clean several hundred boats. In addition to hull cleanings, we provide underwater inspections, search & recovery, salvage, anode replacement and a variety of other underwater services. While the work is not intellectually stimulating, it is still invigorating and not at all boring. On some level I actually enjoy it. Perhaps it is the peaceful quiet of working underwater or maybe it is the fact I am being paid to do something I love – diving.

You may be surprised to learn that the Baltimore Harbor is full of marine life. It is not unusual to see a variety of fish on a single dive, from white perch to striped bass, catfish to blue crabs, American eels to menhaden and more. The summer also brings a few varieties of jellyfish and the things we're usually there to clean up – the barnacles and mussels.

There are many large marinas in Baltimore and we work in all of them. The most common question my employees and I hear is "Are you really going to get in that water?" You see the perception of the harbor is that it is terribly polluted. The fact is, that while years of industry deposited copious amounts of chromium and other metals into the harbor and the Jones and Gwynn's falls' deposit huge amounts of debris, such as plastic bags, bottles, cans etc…, and occasionally raw sewage

Ken Barrick

leaks in, the harbor is reasonably clean and accommodates life quite well.

I often make fun of OSHA regulations that require public safety divers to wear full encapsulation because the water is so "toxic." I have been diving in the Baltimore Harbor thousands of times over the past decade and I have never developed anything more than a slight ear infection, something I routinely contracted while swimming in the local high school and college pools. In addition, I have been tested for exposure to heavy metals and the results have been negative. My employees and I are vaccinated for hepatitis and tetanus. Historically these were the only two things we ever worried about, until one very special day.

I remember it very clearly. I was standing on the dock speaking with the boat owner, my client, while one of my divers, Ryan, was in the water working on cleaning the running gear of a large power boat. Suddenly a school of striped bass, known locally as rockfish began leaping out of the water and landing on the dock. All around us were striped bass. The boat owner and I glanced at each other with a puzzled look and began kicking them back into the water. In that moment I remember thinking to myself, this is the oddest thing I've ever seen.

Before that thought exited my mind, Ryan shot out of the water like a sea lion attempting to avoid the jaws of a great white shark. In full SCUBA equipment, he propelled himself more than eighteen inches high to land his upper torso on the floating dock. He was as pale as a ghost when he looked up at me, eyes larger than quarters – "SH SH SHARK" is all he stuttered.

I looked at him and told him he was full of crap, there were no sharks in the Baltimore Harbor and even if there were, there was no way he saw one while he was working. Visibility that day was less than twelve inches, so for him to have seen it, it would have had to swim right across his face mask. "Get back in the water and finish the job" I ordered, to which he replied "I'm not going back in there, you go finish it."

It was obvious something had scared him. I had never seen him like this. While I did think it was odd that the striped bass were jumping out of the water, my previous experience told me they were probably being chased by a school of the more voracious Bluefish.

As I began pulling on my wetsuit, the striped bass began to jump again, a little farther away from the dock and this time the reason

- 48 -

became clear. There it was, breaching the surface, the dorsal fin of a rather large shark. My knowledge of sharks told me the only species this large likely to be in this brackish water was the ever aggressive bull shark. YES! There was a shark in the Baltimore Harbor.

I finished suiting up and asked Ryan if he was going to get back in and help me finish the job. His answer was "Are you crazy?" While he and the boat owner made jokes about how they would divide my SCUBA gear if I didn't make it back out, I reminded them they'd actually have to get in the water to retrieve it. I knew that the shark was occupied with the striped bass and that I wasn't on his menu. I told Ryan, "If people were on the sharks menu, you would have already been eaten."

Remember, Ryan actually saw the shark while he was working underwater. When I entered the water to finish cleaning the boat, the visibility was in fact less than twelve inches. That shark had swum within a foot of Ryan's head. I spent a lot of time teasing him and telling him he was a sissy, but the fact of the matter is, at least he didn't soil his wetsuit, not that I could tell.

In the years since seeing the shark in the harbor, I am always thinking about being grabbed by a shark as I work in the dark zero visibility. I'm not sure what I worry about more, being grabbed by a shark, or seeing a dead body go floating by.

OH LORD, LET'S ALL JOIN HANDS & PRAY

This is probably my favorite diving story of all time, but it has very little to do with actually diving. Operating a small commercial diving operation has introduced me to some real characters over the years. One of my favorite characters was a very nice old lady named Ms. Benson.

Ms. Henson had been a client of mine for a year or two, occasionally having me come out to clean the bottom of her rickety old, barely floating, houseboat. The boat was in such bad condition that marina management was constantly trying to devise a plan to get her and her boat out of the marina.

My phone rang and I answered it. It was Ms. Henson. She seemed a bit flustered and wasn't quite sure how to approach me with her request. "How can I help you Ms. Henson?" I asked. She replied "Ken, I think I've lost my teeth in the water."

The most important word in her statement was the word "think." You see, she thought she dropped her false teeth in the water, but she wasn't one-hundred percent sure. Now oddly enough this wasn't the first call we had ever received from a customer about dropping their false teeth in the water. We had one other incident where a gentleman had been eating at a waterfront restaurant, or perhaps a better way to describe it, drinking at the waterfront restaurant. He became ill and lost his teeth while vomiting over the balcony.

Getting back to Ms. Henson; "Ms. Henson" I asked, "Why do you think your teeth are in the water?" She quickly informed me that she had walked across the street to the grocery store and purchased some groceries to take back to her boat. When she arrived at her boat, she bent over to sit her bags on the swim platform and she heard something go splash into the water. At first she thought it was some change that fell out of her pocket, but now that she had spent the last hour looking for her false teeth, she remembered that she had taken them out of her mouth and put them in her shirt pocket. "Oh my Ken" she said, "What am I going to do without my teeth?"

I informed her not to worry, perhaps they had, in fact, fallen in the water and if so, I would have them for her in no time. I hung up the phone and headed to the marina.

When I arrived at the marina I donned my gear and jumped in to have a look around where Ms. Henson reported being when she heard the splash. The visibility was amazingly good that day and I remember thinking, if the teeth were in the water, I'd have no trouble finding them.

I spent the better part of thirty minutes searching for those teeth. I was fairly well convinced after the first thirty seconds that the teeth were not in the water, but I wanted to make every effort. My success rate for finding items during search and recovery operations was one-hundred percent at the time and I didn't want a blemish on that stellar record. Eventually I gave up, convinced the teeth were not in the water, and headed to the surface to give Ms. Henson the news.

When I broke the surface of the water I emerged into what I can best describe as looking like an AA meeting. There were seven or eight people standing in a circle staring at me as I broke the surface. I looked up and said "I'm really sorry Ms. Henson, but your teeth are not in this water." As I climbed out, I added "but Ms. Henson, I'm going to say a little prayer for you – that you find your teeth."

Unbeknownst to me, one member of the group standing on the dock was an old black Baptist minister and he threw his hands up in the air and announced "Oh Lord Lets all Join Hands and Pray that Ms. Henson find her teeth." Everyone in the group, my-self included joined hands, staring down at the water and prayed for Ms. Henson to find her teeth.

I gathered up my equipment, packed my truck and headed home. As I opened my front door some thirty minutes later, my telephone was ringing. I rushed to the phone and grabbed it. I noticed on the caller ID that it was Ms. Henson. "Hello Ms. Henson, how may I help you?" I said. "Ken you are never going to believe it." "Did you find your teeth?" I asked; to which Ms. Henson replied "Can you believe it? Ben found my teeth in the middle of Boston Street."

Ben happens to be another of the live-aboard boaters at the marina. He rides his bicycle all over the downtown area and on this particular day he had been riding on Boston Street in the area of the grocery store Ms. Henson had visited. When Ben arrived back at the marina, he saw the large group gathered and had stopped to ask them what was going on. He was informed that Ms. Henson had lost her false teeth, to which he replied "That's funny, I just saw some false teeth in the middle of Boston Street."

Ben rode his bike back to the location and recovered the teeth. They were in fact Ms. Henson's! As Ms. Henson finished telling me the glorious story, only one thing came to mind. I said "You see Ms. Henson, that's the power of prayer!" We had a good laugh and the day ended well.

This is a fun true story but for me the real story is how powerful prayer can be. The chance that her teeth were found in the middle of Baltimore City, and even more-so not run over by a car and destroyed, given that they were in the middle of a heavily traveled city street for more than an hour, is no small miracle. These are magical words I'll never have a problem repeating… "Oh Lord, Lets All Join Hands and Pray!"

BILLY'S BOULDER

Bonaire in the Netherlands Antilles' is considered by many to be the shore diving capital of the world. In Bonaire, you jump into a vehicle, drive around the island and stop to dive wherever you see a marker. The markers are painted rocks and they indicate a shore entry spot for one of the many mapped dive site locations.

I had never been interested in diving Bonaire. I considered it beneath me. Everyone I knew who had been there raved about how "easy" the diving was. All of the senior citizen divers I knew made annual treks there. It sounded to me like Bonaire was the old age home for divers.

My friend Mel had booked a trip to Bonaire and had a large group of divers going. He asked Michelle and me if we'd like to go along. I really wasn't thrilled with the aspects of diving there, but it was a big group, many of whom I liked and enjoyed spending time with, so I said yes.

Upon arrival, Louie's Dive Resort seemed like a nice enough place. The resort employees were friendly and it had a "house" reef that you could dive anytime day or night. The resort was highly recommended by many, but it ended up being the vacation from hell for quite a few of our travelers, Mel included.

During the week we were at Louie's, Mel fell down some very slippery steps and injured his back. Several of our guests had dive equipment stolen from their rooms. A handful of people became ill from food poisoning, we assumed, since they had all eaten the same meals. One guest and his wife fell off a rented scooter and had to go to the hospital when the scooter's brakes failed. On top of all this, there was the constant noise from construction at the resort. The crews were literally jack-hammering all day, and finally, there is the story of Billy's

Boulder which has a much better ending than we could possibly have hoped for on this trip.

For most of the week, Mel, Billy, Michelle and I along with a newly certified couple, piled into our rental van and drove around the island. We dove several sites with varying degrees of enjoyment. One day, one of the resort dive masters told us about a fairly private dive site, one that was no longer visited on a regular basis and was really only dove by island locals. We decided to check it out.

Over the mountains and through the woods we went to find this dive site. At the end of our journey we came to a private residence with a small beach in front of it. We could see a man fishing in a wooden dinghy just off shore. The scene was truly rustic. It was the second time I remember being on an island and literally feeling like I was at the end of the earth. The other time was on the island of Bimini, when I was actually at a bar called "The End of the World."

The six of us donned our equipment and entered the water. The first thing we saw was a massive six foot long Barracuda, perhaps the largest Barracuda I have ever seen. The dive site was pristine. The water was perhaps the clearest in all of Bonaire. Various colors of blue danced around me and there was a vibrancy I had not observed at any of the other dive sites.

Mel and I were the most experienced divers in the group of six and so we had made an agreement. Throughout the week of diving we would take turns leading and bringing up the rear. On this dive, I was the lead diver. I would be responsible for getting us out and back and making sure we turned around at the appropriate time for our biggest ASP (air sucking pig), i.e. the diver who used their air the fastest.

I have always hated to lead, and this dive once again showed why. As the leader, you miss everything that happens behind you. What I am about to tell you is the story as told to me by my wife and verified by Mel and the freshly minted dive couple. Billy pleaded the fifth.

Our good friend Billy is a self described ASP. He is also a budding underwater photographer. On this dive, I was out in front leading, followed by Billy and Michelle, then the young couple, and Mel was bringing up the rear, at least that is what I thought. We reached a beautiful area of the dive where the wall dropped down pretty significantly. Unbeknownst to me, was that Billy had stopped to take a photo and my wife had stopped with him (she too was taking photos of the same subject matter), allowing Mel and the young couple to "catch up" so to say.

Apparently Billy decided to lean his camera (and his body weight) on a large coral boulder in an attempt to take a photo. In doing so he dislodged the boulder from the wall and it began rolling down the side of the wall leaving behind it a path of destruction. As Mel swam along beneath Billy's position, he was unknowing of the danger he faced, the boulder heading straight for him.

My wife frantically tried to signal Mel to alert him to the coming danger, but to no avail. The boulder went by Mel's head, passing just in front of him and missing by inches. Everyone saw it except me. I swore afterward that this was the last dive I was leading.

Luckily the story has a happy ending. The boulder missed crushing Mel's head, and because it passed in front of him, he got to see it. Meanwhile Billy got a new nickname "Boulder Bill." My wife and the new divers got a great show and a scare, and all I got was the chance to write this damn story. I love listening to Mel tell the story of how this huge boulder just missed his head, it is hysterical.

The rest of the dive was fairly uneventful, but as with all stories it doesn't end as expected. We exited the water and packed our gear back into the van. Just as we were getting ready to pull off, the old man from the fishing boat pulls up next to us on a golf cart. He was waving his hand for us to come and look at what he caught. He was smiling and excited as he unrolled a large white towel to unveil that massive Barracuda we had observed at the start of our dive. We politely smiled and waved back to him. He didn't speak any English and we couldn't understand what he was saying, but it was disappointing to see that beautiful animal, that had been swimming with us and who had lived so long, wrapped in that towel. I nearly cried.

EXHAUST PIPE

When I first started writing this book I never thought I'd be telling stories about my dive business, KB Diver Services. I anticipated that I'd be telling you about my grand adventures travelling around the world, but as I sat at my desk writing, I realized both were equally entertaining.

I received a call from a local waterfront homeowner who asked if I could come find an exhaust cover that had fallen off his boat. He lived just five minutes from my home on the same creek. I asked him for details and he informed me he had banged the bottom of his boat on his lift as he was docking. He noticed the exhaust cover was missing once the boat was lifted and in place. He said that the cover could only be in one place, in the water straight down beneath the lift, within a couple feet, give or take. This was going to be the easiest one hundred dollar bill I'd ever made. I told him I would stop by on my way home in the afternoon to retrieve the exhaust cover.

Bert, one of my trusted divers, was working with me that day. While Bert is excellent at boat maintenance work and has become quite comfortable cleaning boats in zero visibility, he had not conducted searches for me. After a long day of work, I decided to break Bert in and give him one of the easiest search and recovery jobs I had ever been called for. I would go along to advise him and also be there to complete the task if he somehow failed.

The water in the creek beneath the boat lift was only five or six feet deep. The lift was of course connected to the homeowner's private pier and so there were also several pilings to use as reference points. The exhaust cover was missing from the port side of the boat, which was the side closest to the pier. Assuming the boat had banged into the lift as positioned, there was only one place this cover could be; about two feet off the pier and straight down in five feet of water.

Given how shallow the water was, it would have been possible to jump in and walk around until your foot hit the exhaust cover, then simply bend over and pick it up, but that would have been too easy. I wanted Bert to gain search experience in the easiest possible setting, so I had him gear up. I showed him how to drop a reference line attached to an anchor straight down where the exhaust cover was expected to be. I call this the target point.

Bert dropped the line where I told him. I then advised him to use it as a descent line and that once he got to the bottom, to feel around with his hands, locate and retrieve the exhaust cover and bring it to the surface. It literally had to be within an arms' reach of the reference line.

Bert entered the water and put his face down. He looked back up at me and said "I can't see anything." I told him not to worry, just hold onto the descent line and don't let go. I remember telling him specifically "If you let go of that line, you're not going to have any idea where you are."

Down he went. I expected him to literally hit his head on the exhaust cover, pick it up and be back in less than thirty seconds. As I watched his bubbles I counted, one minute, two minutes, three minutes, then his bubbles started moving. First they went under the pier, then back out, then away from the pier and then suddenly toward the middle of the creek. Oh crap!

Bert had obviously let go of the reference line and he was now headed into the middle of the creek. It was a busy afternoon on the water and boats were headed straight for his bubbles. While I knew he was on the bottom, the maximum depth in the creek was only about nine feet. He was in danger of being shredded by the large powerboats headed straight for him. There was no way the boats could see him.

I frantically jumped and waved at the boats but to no avail. I was standing there in just my bathing suit, but I had no choice, the only way to save Bert was to put myself in harms' way, and in more ways than one. I jumped into the water and swam towards Bert's bubbles. There was a slight current, but I had two thoughts in mind. One was to reach Bert before the boats did, dive down, grab him and yank him back to the surface. My other thought was – If I stayed on the surface, the boaters would see me and stop. I waived my arms at the approaching boats using the international sign for distress. They didn't seem to see me. I dove down reaching for Bert but missed in the darkness. I tried again and again I missed.

When I popped back up the second time I heard the boats engines powering down. Thank God someone on the first boat saw me in the water. I yelled to him, asking him to use his boat to block the other boats coming behind him and he complied. I relocated Bert's bubbles and made one last effort to grab him. Success! I grabbed him and pulled him to the surface.

There we were, in the middle of the creek. Me with no mask, fins, snorkel or anything else, held up by adrenaline, and there was Bert, with this goofy look on his face like "How did I get out here?" I wanted to smack him so hard, you just don't know.

I yelled a big thank you to the boater and we headed back to the pier. Once we arrived, Bert asked if he should try again to retrieve the exhaust cover. I told him "Hell no! Get your rear end out of this water right now." I could not believe what I had just seen. He had damn near got us both killed because he didn't follow a simple direction – DON'T LET GO OF THE LINE!

Once he was out of the water and safely back on land, I swam over to the line, took a deep breath of air and descended straight down the entire depth of five feet. When I put my hand down to brace myself it landed squarely on something hard and heavy. A rock I thought, but as I moved my hand around the contour it became clear it was man-made. It was the exhaust cover, literally right next to the reference line anchor. I grabbed it and struggled to get it to the surface. That little bugger must have weighed ten pounds. It was pretty hard to bring up.

I handed the exhaust cover to Bert and climbed up the ladder. He seemed dumbfounded. "Where did you find that?" he asked. "Right next to the line" I replied. He asked me if it was that big hard thing down there. "Yep, that was it" I said.

It seems he had landed on it just like I did, but he dismissed it as "a rock or something." I can't say I blame him, I almost made the same mistake, but I can blame him for letting go of the line and damn near getting us both killed. Needless to say, Bert has not conducted any more searches since that fateful day, several years ago. On occasion I jokingly ask him if he'd like to try another search, to which he simply replies "Remember what happened last time?"

I went home that night replaying the scene over and over in my head. Should I have done anything differently? My wife gave the best answer, "Yeah, you should have done the search yourself."

LEAP OF FAITH III

How many leaps of faith can one man take and still be alive to tell about them? I promise this is the last "leap of faith" story.

West coast diving is different than east coast diving, for many reasons. Most west coast divers dive the west coast of the United States and west toward Asia and most east coast divers dive the east coast and east into the Caribbean. If they have anything in common, it is that both coast's divers head north and south.

My first trip to do west coast diving is one I will never forget. Michelle had a great job that afforded her terrific travel opportunities. On occasion, I was able to travel with her. One such trip took us to San Diego, California. If you have never been to San Diego, trust me when I tell you, it is one of the prettiest cities in the United States.

We didn't know anyone who had been diving in San Diego and were completely unfamiliar with the local diving opportunities. I did a little research online and found an operator called Pacific Escape. I called and told them that my wife and I were experienced divers from Baltimore and we were looking to do a couple of dives while visiting San Diego. "No problem," they said, "we've got room on the boat for you."

When we arrived at the dive shop we were greeted by a friendly employee who helped fit us for our wetsuits and loaded up our gear bags. He gave us the information we needed on where to find the boat and off we went, still not sure what to expect.

When we arrived at the boat we were told by the Captain he had a large group of Open Water diving students onboard along with their Instructor. He told us the boat was heading out to a shallow area of the Coronado Islands where the open water checkout dives were conducted with students. He apologized to us and told us that it probably wasn't the best day for us to be on the boat. We were kind of bummed out. The dive shop had not informed us that we were going out with students on a shallow "check out" dive.

On the way to the dive site the captain called Michelle and I over and asked another couple to join us. He informed us that we were all experienced divers and that if we were game, he would do something special for us. He continued on telling us that if we were interested, he would have us do a military (high speed) roll off the side of the boat and then continue on a drift dive along the island. He told us we would be able to find the boat, instructor and students by making a right turn at the "big rock." He informed us that we'd like this dive much better than going with the instructor and his students, who would be sitting in the sand reviewing diving skills.

Michelle asked him what we would see if we followed his plan and he replied there was a good chance of seeing sea lions, garibaldi and different sea stars as well as some patches of kelp that housed other smaller fish. The wife from the other couple asked about the roll off the boat and he said it had to be done this way in order to get us close enough to the island while at the same time keeping the boat off the rocks below.

I looked at Michelle and she looked at me and together we looked at the other couple, "What the hell," I said, "you only live once." They agreed.

As the Captain slowed the boat and we prepared to "go, go, go, go" in our military rolls off the starboard side, I remember looking around just before I jumped, wondering if I had lost my mind. I didn't know this Captain. I didn't know this other couple. I didn't know this dive site. What if I somehow missed the big rock? What exactly did they mean by the big rock? Then it dawned on me that I was in California and there were great white sharks in southern California. Then I remembered him mentioning sea lions. I thought to myself, great whites feed on sea lions. Suddenly the signal came "Go, Go, Go, Go..." I jumped in and watched the boat speed away into the distance. I remember thinking I had lost my mind.

I located Michelle, which wasn't easy in the three to four foot chop. Together we looked around for the other couple but did not see them. I assumed they had already descended and so I signaled to Michelle to do the same. Down we went.

The visibility was pretty good and as we approached the bottom, I remember thinking "pretty cool." Suddenly a large sea lion came out of nowhere and headed at rocket speed right for Michelle's mid section. Just at the last second it veered away, scaring the crap out of her. She would later say her heart skipped a beat. We ended up seeing one or two more sea lions on the dive, which was exciting, since these were the first ones we had ever observed in the water.

On occasion I'd look around for the other couple, but never saw them the entire dive. I started to become consumed with where they were. Then I became consumed with the big rock. Where was this big rock? What if we missed it and didn't make the turn?

We had taken quite a leap of faith. We were in the middle of the Pacific Ocean, in a location we were not familiar with, diving with another couple we couldn't find, from a boat we had no previous experience with. What flashed into my mind next was that we had rented equipment from Pacific Escape, so at least they would look for us if their equipment didn't make it back. That gave me some comfort, as well as the fact we were diving along the side of an island. The worst case scenario may be that we ended up stranded on the island for a couple of days. I went back to looking for some garibaldi's and starfish.

All my fears were settled and my prayers answered when suddenly a huge rock came into view and there was a corner to turn. This had to be the big rock. It was huge. I signaled to Michelle and we began our right turn around the rock. There they were, just as the captain said they would be, the group of students kneeling in a circle on the bottom. I could clearly see the anchor line of the boat and the knot in my stomach finally began to loosen.

The dive was great. All the anxiety vanished and I realized that one more time I had taken a leap of faith and survived. All was good in my world and I would do this dive again any day.

Once back onboard the boat we found the other couple. They too had made it back and enjoyed their dive, but the best was yet to come. The captain came out of the cabin with a huge pot of piping hot chili, some fruit and some drinks. The water temperature in California is always mid-fifties or so. I don't know if it was the best chili I've eaten or not, but it sure was on that day. We thanked the captain for allowing us to do the dive and for his amazing chili, which he was proud to tell us, he made all by himself.

ONE STUDENT

As a SCUBA Instructor, my favorite thing to do is work with private students. The students gain so much more from this type of interaction and they always become better divers more quickly than in a large class setting. I think most instructors will agree with that statement and most instructors fancy taking these types of jobs whenever the opportunity arises.

A few years ago I had two dive students signed up for an Advanced Navigation class. I could have easily handled them myself, but I had a fellow instructor itching to teach some advanced classes. I called him and offered him one of my advanced navigation students. He was thrilled, so we set a date and planned to work together getting the two students completed.

On a beautiful Wednesday evening we headed to Bainbridge Quarry, one of many local spots we use for training. I assigned my fellow instructor to work with Gary, a former Baltimore City Police Officer and former military retiree. I would be working with the other student. The plan was for the two students to do team navigation and then move on to navigating on their own, followed, of course, by their individual instructor to ensure safety.

The two students performed brilliantly on their team navigation. Team navigation requires one person to navigate using the compass and the other team member to monitor depth keeping the team leveled off at an assigned depth throughout the duration of the dive.

After running a simple out and back pattern as a team, they successfully completed both triangular and square patterns. It became time to break them apart and challenge them with solo navigation, which required them to stay on course and at a pre-assigned depth without assistance.

I told Tom, my fellow instructor, to have Gary run a solo triangle and to tag along beside or behind him on the same heading to ensure he was not getting too far off course. If he did get off course, Tom was to stop him, let him know he was off course and if necessary have him surface and begin again. I was going to stay on shore with my student until the two of them returned safely from their navigation trial.

Being a SCUBA instructor is both rewarding and challenging, especially in the Northeast United States. Our training quarries can be extremely cold and extremely murky, with visibility often dropping to a few feet or even a few inches during training. We like to tell our students "If you can dive here, you can dive anywhere," and that is very true. We not only have to teach students the required skills for courses, we also have to keep them motivated mentally and physically in extreme conditions such as cold water and limited visibility. Most Northeast SCUBA instructors are highly skilled professionals, but given the high degree of difficulty, sometimes strange events such as this one, occur.

Gary was set to run his triangle pattern with Tom following. If all went well, they would end up back on shore within a few feet of where my student and I waited. Gary took his initial compass heading and together, he and Tom, began their descent from the water's edge. My student and I watched as their bubbles breached the water's surface as they made their way. They were to swim forty kick cycles during each leg of the triangular pattern. After each length they would stop to turn the required one-hundred twenty degrees until they returned to shore.

A strange thing happened at end of the first length. As we watched from shore, we could see the two sets of bubbles separating. One went to the left and the other just seemed to be hovering in place moving very little. I was perplexed. I felt good knowing there were still two sets of bubbles, this at least indicated both divers were still alive and breathing, but it was obvious that they were no longer together. My student and I watched as one set of bubbles continued on what appeared to be a perfect second leg of the triangular pattern while the other was still not moving. Which diver was where? The bigger question in my mind was how did this experienced dive instructor lose an experienced single student? In addition, I wondered why neither diver had surfaced to search for his buddy. Even though the student was in fact a student, he was still a certified open water diver who should know to surface if he became separated from his dive buddy. My biggest concern was that one set of bubbles was moving and the other seemed to be stuck in place.

Ken following a navigation student – Bahamas (Photo by Michelle Barrick)

The set of bubbles that was moving had turned the corner and was on its final approach to shore. As the diver stood up, I was amazed to see it was Gary the student. He had completed a perfect triangle pattern. I immediately asked him where his buddy was, to which he replied "I don't know, behind me I guess."

At this point I was worried. Just as I was telling both students to hang tight on shore while I went to find Tom, Tom surfaced, still in the same place he had been while Gary completed his compass run. I told Gary to duck behind us so Tom could not see him and I yelled to Tom "Where is your student?"

Tom looked around the water's surface for bubbles but didn't see any. He yelled back "I don't know!" It was both funny and sad. I could not understand how he had lost just one student. I yelled back "What do you mean you don't know where he is?"

I watched Tom frantically look around for any sign of bubbles. I could not resist watching him squirm for just a few more minutes. I could sense panic in his voice when he yelled to me "Ken, we need to look for him," to which I replied, "No we don't, he's right here on shore!"

As Tom shook his head and began the swim back to meet us, I begged the students to ask him one question when he got back, "Tom, how in the hell do you lose just one student?" They asked, and we all had a good laugh at Tom's expense. Thank goodness everything turned out okay. Myself and a few of my fellow instructors love to rag on Tom about this incident, but the fact of the matter is, losing one student is not all that difficult to do when the visibility is just a few inches.

THE STORIES OF TWO PLANES

Traveling around the world SCUBA diving has inherent risks. There are the obvious risks related specifically to SCUBA, such as decompression sickness, lung over-expansion injuries, attacks by marine life, etc..., and then there are the other risks.

One of the other risks is unrest in foreign countries. I was in Utila, just after the Honduran military overthrew the elected president and I was visiting a resort in Roatan when six heavily armed Honduran soldiers came running through the courtyard chasing a drug smuggler. In addition, there are risks from drinking bad water, malaria, having access to only sub-standard medical care etc...

Very few people consider their chosen mode of transportation a major risk. We all know that airplanes crash on occasion, trains derail, etc..., but none of us ever expects these things to happen to us. I honestly think the most fascinating thing about this book is the fact that I'm still here to write it. Let me explain.

Many years ago my wife and I joined a group of divers from Aqua Ventures in Cockeysville, Maryland on a diving vacation to San Salvador Island Bahamas. Still to this day, I remember this story as if it occurred just yesterday.

We flew from Baltimore to Miami on the first leg of our journey. We then had to make an overnight stay in Miami before boarding our puddle jumper flight the next morning. I'm not sure which scared me more, the overnight stay in Miami or the flight the next morning.

After arriving in Miami and checking into our beach front hotel, my wife and I decided to take a nice evening stroll on the beach. As I was holding her hand and trying to be romantic by giving her a little kiss on the cheek, my eyes wandered to one of the most heinous sites I have ever seen. There in plain view was a naked hairy four hundred pound man sitting in a beach chair with his legs spread wide open and a big old smile on his face. He even waved to me. I cringed, closed my eyes and turned my wife and myself in the opposite direction, but it was too late. She and I had seen him in all his glory.

We laughed our rear ends off as we headed down the beach in the opposite direction. I had no idea we were on a nude beach. There were very few people on the beach and most had clothing on, but I soon figured out what was going on. A man who had been swimming just off shore began to walk up out of the water several yards in front of us. He too was naked, and his man parts were dangling in the breeze like an Adam and Eve wind-chime. I stopped and covered my wife's poor eyes as I took another look. I laughed so hard I thought I was going to have a stroke. Luckily it didn't kill me. I lived to make the flight the next morning.

We awoke early, excited about the day ahead. We planned to arrive on the island early in the afternoon and have some nice beach time before sitting down to dinner at the Riding Rock Inn. Our group of sixteen had to be divided into two groups of eight to make the flight over to San Salvador. We had two eight-seat twin-prop airplanes to choose from.

Once aboard the airplane, the pilots positioned each member of our group in an attempt to distribute the weight evenly. My wife was stuck in the very last single row seat next to the luggage. I was seated just two rows behind the pilots, which gave me a good view of the instrument cluster. This would be important later on.

The plane took off without incident and we made our gradual climb to cruising altitude. About half way into the flight, I was tapped on the shoulder by my "seat buddy" and asked this disturbing question, "Should there be oil leaking from the engine?" I peeped around him and observed a very discernable flow of blackish fluid coming from the propeller. I looked over the shoulders of the couple in front of me and could see the two engine gauges on the instrument cluster. The needle on left gauge was in the red and the one on the right was in the black. I could hear the pilots talking but I couldn't make out what they were saying.

The next thing I knew, the plane began descending. It was a controlled descent, but I knew something was going on when I looked out the window and could see the water. The water was so close I felt everything would be okay. I remember thinking to myself; we're flying low enough that if the plane goes down, we'll simply climb out and put on our SCUBA gear.

My seat buddy and I discussed whether we should say anything to our fellow travelers. We could tell that no one else noticed what was happening. They were all either sleeping or simply didn't have a view of the engine leak. I looked back at my wife and flashed a smile. I didn't know whether I should be worried or not. The plane did have two engines and two pilots. We decided to keep our mouths shut. There was no reason to alarm anyone.

After what seemed like an eternity, the plane finally landed. I walked over to the two pilots who were conversing with each other and mentioned the engine leak. One looked at me, smiled, paused and thought about his choice of words – "This plane isn't going anywhere for a very long time" he said. The other pilot looked a little more shaken and said, "I'm sure as hell not flying it." I wasn't really sure what to say to them, so I kept it short and simple, "Good job guys – thanks for getting us here in one piece." They smiled and nodded and I went on my way. It wasn't until our group was in the bus on the way to the resort that my seat buddy and I agreed to tell everyone what had occurred. It was then that one of my fellow travelers, a gentleman who had visited San Sal on a previous vacation, informed us of a wreck site we may dive during the week. It's called "The Runway" and is actually an airplane similar to the one we had just arrived on. It is several hundred yards off shore, just in front of the airport runway. It is another small dual-prop airplane that didn't quite make it to the island. I remember thinking to myself "Now they tell me!"

My second airplane story occurred in Honduras. My wife and I had been scheduled to travel with another group from Aqua Ventures, but the week of our scheduled trip, Hurricane Mitch decided to wreak havoc in the Bay Islands. The group trip was canceled and rescheduled a few months later, but my wife and I could not travel that week and ended up rescheduling alone.

We had some minor reservations about traveling to Honduras on our own, but we figured it would be okay. How different could it be from traveling with a large group? We soon found out.

The runway on Roatan had been washed out during Hurricane Mitch and was still not operational for larger airplanes when we made our journey. This forced our flight to be routed onto the mainland of Honduras to a town called San Pedro Sula. We did some research and found that San Pedro Sula was not the friendliest place on earth. We were told not to leave the airport, not to wear or carry anything expensive and whatever we did, not to look the armed airport guards (the Honduran Army) in the eye. All of this made me feel warm and fuzzy inside.

It was pre-9/11, and my foreign travel experience before this trip was fairly limited. It came as a shock to me when I stepped off a large modern airplane onto a staircase leading to the tarmac. At the bottom of the steps were members of the Honduran Army, armed with automatic rifles. They were everywhere and apparently they were needed to secure the airport from rebels. Remembering what I was told, I put my head down and marched pass them as if I was trying to hide my size and strength. My wife and I made it into the airport, collected our bags and attempted to figure out what we were supposed to do next.

It was an airport like any other, only smaller and more disorganized. We had connecting flight information, but we found out that our plane had already left for the day. It was the only commercial flight from San Pedro Sula to Roatan. Luckily we were able to communicate with our ticketing agent. She spoke fluent English. She advised us that we had two choices and she would be happy to assist us with either option. The first option was to get a hotel in San Pedro Sula for the evening and be back at the airport to catch the commercial flight the next day around noon. The second option was to fly over to Roatan on a "local" flight which was leaving in about an hour.

Remembering what I had been told about San Pedro Sula and the fact that the Army was needed to secure the airport from rebels, it didn't take long for my wife and me to choose the "local" flight. The ticket agent advised us she would alert our resort that we were coming and they would send someone to the airport on Roatan to pick us up. This sounded like a winner.

Not long after receiving our tickets the announcement came that our flight was boarding. We walked through the doorway as directed and onto the tarmac. An attractive young Honduran woman directed us to our plane. As we walked toward it a line began to form. There were people holding everything from small children to small dogs and even chickens. One woman had a large rat-like creature native to the island. As I got closer to the airplane itself, I inspected it. It was a twin-prop plane and looked as if it would hold forty or fifty people. It had no markings on it whatsoever, it was just a large plain white airplane and not as clean as I was used to flying on.

My wife and I took our assigned seats. As we waited, two guys wearing white shirts and blue jeans walked up the aisle toward the cockpit; to this day I swear one of them had a Budweiser can in his hand. A few minutes later, first in Spanish and then in broken English, the Pilot announces "We need all the big people move to the back of the plane. We have to get nose of plane up to make it over the mountain, or we hit mountain." Now I was getting nervous.

I tried to stay by my wife's side, but one of the attendants tapped my shoulder and motioned for me to follow her. She reseated me in the back of the plane. It was about this time that I noticed the chaos in front of me. There were chickens hopping from one seat to another and young children trying to grab them. A dog was barking and there were more people on this plane than there were seats.

The interior lights went out and the exterior lights came on. The flight was taking off just as the sun was setting and most of this short flight would be in the dark of night. I looked out of my window and could see the mountain ahead. I closed my eyes and said a prayer.

As the plane rumbled down the runway, it seemed heavy. I didn't think we were going to lift off, much less make it over the mountain. I remember waiting for the pilot to slam on the brakes and start over, but suddenly we lifted off. The mountain in front of me seemed perilously close and with a long way up to make it over. The next thing I knew it felt like I was in a space shuttle. There I was looking straight up, with the feeling of being on my back. The airplane was vertical! It seemed like minutes, but was probably just seconds before the plane began leveling off.

I heard the cackle of the pilot's microphone and in a very jubilant tone he broke the dead silence with "Woooooooohoooo that was a close one!" The Honduran locals aboard cheered and celebrated the success. Apparently not all locals are so lucky.

I said a second prayer that ended with "Thank you Jesus." Now we were over the mountain, but we still needed to fly over the water and land this plane on the washed out island runway. A short time later the wheels touched the ground and we walked off the airplane. I gave my wife a big hug and told her we were on an adventure. "Welcome to Roatan," called out the resort employee who had come to pick us up, "Glad you made it!" I remember looking him straight in the eye and telling him – "So are we!"

Ken Barrick

DID YOU KNOW?

There are tens of millions of certified SCUBA divers living throughout the world. Some of these divers are marine biologist and scientist, but most are just average everyday human beings with a sense of adventure. I definitely fall into the latter category. I earned a D in high school biology and never even attempted a science class during my short time in college. Prior to becoming a diver, the only thing I found entertaining about science had occurred in tenth grade. My project mate was a kid named Robin Borgmann and together we became known as Doctors Barrick & Borgmann, famous for the constant pranks we played on our biology teacher.

During the dissection of a frog we neatly connected parts of the frog together that did not belong together, then called our teacher over to ask why our frog looked different than everyone else's. As she stood there looking over our shoulder, scratching her head and searching for an answer, we burst out laughing. She didn't find it amusing at all.

During another experiment, when she insisted there was absolutely no way to get a bloodworm out of a straw if it didn't want to come out, we connected the straw to a high pressure water system and blasted the worm across the classroom where it grossly went splat on the chalkboard. We showed her.

So to say I'm a scientist is a stretch, but I will say I have observed certain things during my years of diving that give me a leg up on the scientist. I am proud to say I have even documented some of these occurrences on video tape.

My first observance involves a nurse shark. As a diver, I refer to these sharks as the puppy dogs of the sea. They are usually shy but can be curious and they are not considered much of a danger to divers.

Nurse sharks lack the razor sharp teeth shared by most other shark species, instead having teeth made for crushing. There are numerous stories of nurse sharks clamping on to humans and not letting go, even so, they are not considered a threat.

While diving in Little Cayman, I happened upon a nurse shark sleeping in a crevice on the ledge of a wall. Holding my video camera I moved slowly toward the shark. I didn't want to startle it, because if it felt trapped, it may charge directly at me. It really didn't have anywhere to move except forward and I was in its path.

I'm not sure what alerted the shark to my presence, but I assume it was the bubbles from my regulator. The shark wagged its head back and forth, similar to what a bull does just before charging at rodeo clowns. "Oh crap!" I thought "This shark is not happy with me."

I started to slowly back away and that's when I learned something about nurse sharks I had never heard of or read before. The shark began using its pectoral fins to walk backward. It took three or four "steps," backing away from me as I backed away from it. As the shark moved, it pushed rocks and shells out of its way using its pectoral fins.

Nurse shark walking backward (Photo by Ken Barrick)

All the science I had ever read indicated sharks moved in only one direction, forward. In fact, most species had to move forward constantly to survive. Some, but very few could lie motionless for periods of time.

Never had it been mentioned sharks could "walk" backward. I'm not sure how many other divers have experienced this, but no one I know has and no one I know, except me, has it captured on video. Chalk one up for my scientific endeavors.

Did you know that sharks sneeze? There is still some debate about this one as well. I have video footage of what I believe to be the only documented evidence of a shark sneezing. It happened by chance in Truk Lagoon.

Diving at a site called "Sharks Pass," I was kneeling on the bottom with my fellow divers shooting video. There were a large number of Black Tip and Grey Reef sharks circling around us. I just kept spinning with the sharks, refocusing, zooming in and out trying to capture some cool images. To be honest, my time in the water was a blur. I really wasn't sure what I was capturing on film, I just kept shooting.

It wasn't until I returned home and sat down at my computer to edit the footage that I discovered my clip of a shark sneezing. I replayed the clip ten times before I could convince myself. I had never heard of a shark sneezing, but this sure looked like a shark sneezing to me.

Black tip shark sneezing – Truk Lagoon (Photo by Ken Barrick)

I went online and searched for various forms of "shark sneeze." I used multiple search engines. I found only one obscure note in a much larger article that read "scientists believe sharks sneeze, but there is no documented evidence." Wow I thought - I may have the documented evidence! For the second time in my life, I felt I had captured something of importance with my video camera.

One of the other things I've learned over the years is that Grouper (the fish) can be trained and they are just as smart as dogs. I have fascinating video of this as well.

On my trip to Little Cayman I watched the resort dive master repeatedly call Grouper to her, get them to approach her for a kiss and even hunt for her. She would point to a hole in the reef and the Grouper would swim to the hole and hang out waiting for something to come out. These same Grouper would follow divers around until someone would stop and take the time to pet them. I decided to try working with the Grouper myself. I wanted to see if they only responded to the dive master or if they were so well trained, anyone could command them.

I spent a minute or two petting the Grouper and then pointed toward a hole in the reef. The Grouper looked at me, started toward the hole, then stopped and came back. I wagged my finger in a scolding no motion, then I pointed at the hole again. The second time the Grouper went to the hole and waited. I couldn't believe it. I had command of the seas creatures. I was all powerful. I was a god in heaven.

Trained grouper with dive master (photo by Ken Barrick)

So did you know that sharks could walk backward, sneeze or that Grouper were intelligent? I have personally witnessed moray eels fighting over a hole, a damselfish attacking a turtle, fish mating and exchanging eggs via mouth, cleaning stations where cleaner shrimp provide dental services to Lizardfish and much more. These are amazing experiences and each and every one of them reminds me how fascinating our planet truly is.

ALMOST DONE

Given all the great times I've had diving, would you believe they almost never happened? It's true, I nearly quit after my very first ocean dive experience.

In the days leading up to the trip my anxiety levels had soared. I had just completed my Open Water SCUBA Diver certification and was now licensed to dive! I didn't have time or money for an exotic vacation, but I lived in Maryland, just three hours from the Atlantic Ocean, and I had heard the Fenwick Shoals was a nice place to start.

Michelle and I signed up for a two-tank dive on the *Surface Interval*, a boat running out of the Indian River Inlet, just north of the Maryland – Delaware line. It seemed to be a close, easy, and inexpensive way to gain some experience. The boat ride was short and the depth was only thirty-five feet to the bottom. This was shallower then my training dives in the quarry.

A couple weeks before the trip, Michelle and I were asked if we would be interested in taking a spear-fishing class and completing our required check out dives aboard the *Surface Interval*. The price was right, and it sounded like fun, so we signed up.

On the morning of the trip I awoke to a light breeze and beautiful sunshine. I loaded our dive gear into the car while Michelle filled the cooler with the day's eats and drinks. I was nervous, but I was ready. Open ocean here I come!

We boarded the boat as our fellow divers' jostled gear about and the banter was heavy on the days plan. Some of the experienced shoals divers were telling stories of their previous exploits, a twenty-two inch flounder, a huge sea bass and monster black drum. Something told me the stories being tossed about were bigger than the fish that had been caught.

I assembled my dive gear, nervously fidgeting, checking then double checking, as all new divers do. Michelle kept telling me to relax until I finally heeded her words. I found a seat in the morning sun, removed my shirt, and basked in the warmth slowly spreading across my skin. I closed my eyes and visualized my first giant stride entry into the sea. My anxiety seemed to fade. Finally I was relaxed.

The boat puttered to a stop and the crew set the anchor. The call came for everyone to gear up, the moment of truth was now upon me, and I was going to be a diver.

It was a warm spring day, unusually warm in fact. The air temperature was ninety degrees and the water temperature a mere fifty. I struggled with the burden of my thick 7mm farmer John wetsuit. I hoisted up the thirty pound weight belt it would take to sink me, slipped on my SCUBA unit, and waited... and waited... and waited. The sweat began to drip from my brow and it didn't take long for me to feel the effects of the glaring sun. The boat rocked in the four foot swells. I could feel my heart beating under my wetsuit; thump, thump, thump. I just wanted to get off the boat.

Finally it was my turn. I grabbed my spear gun and jumped in. I met Michelle on the surface. We gave each other the okay to descend sign and down we went. The visibility was not very good. My best guess was five feet. I struggled with my buoyancy, feeling as if I was being pulled to the surface by a giant vacuum. Even with thirty pounds of lead, I was to light. I was able to stay down, at least for a little while, as I looked for fish in the murky water.

I was anxious about many things. I remember thinking there were twelve other people in the water, all with spear guns, and just five feet of visibility. What if they shot at a fish, and missed, spearing me instead? The lines on the spear shafts were easily fifteen feet in length and you could only see five feet at best. There was no way to know what was beyond your target. For this reason I could not pull the trigger.

I came upon a large boulder and decided to swim over it. This was the first mistake I made in my diving career. As I glided over the top of the boulder I lost control of my buoyancy. The surge monster had me in its grip. I kicked hard toward the bottom in a futile attempt to stop my ascent. The next thing I knew I was on the surface. The seas were choppy with waves three to four feet. I looked around for anything or anyone. I spotted the boat. It looked to me as if it were a mile away. Suddenly Michelle surfaced next to me and asked me what was wrong. I explained that I had been caught in the surge and was unable to stay down. She encouraged me to descend. I tried and tried, but with the air now half depleted from my aluminum tank, I did not have enough weight to counteract the positive buoyancy. I had only one option. I was going to have to surface swim back to the boat.

By now the surface current was carrying us farther from the boat and the wave heights did not allow us to see the boat. I took a compass heading and began my arduous swim. Michelle tried to keep up, but she could not fight the surface current and waves. She informed me she was going to drop beneath the surface and swim underneath me.

Swimming the length of a football field in full SCUBA gear, on the surface, against a current, in four foot waves, in a farmer John wetsuit on a ninety degree day, carrying a long spear gun is no easy task. I didn't think I was going to make it.

My heart was beating fast and hard. Nausea was overtaking me. I was exerting myself unlike any other time in my life. Anxiety almost overtook me, but a strange thing happened. I resigned myself to death. Somehow I found peace with it. I thought to myself "If today is the day, so be it." Oddly enough this gave me some sort of inner stability. I did not panic. Instead I resolved that it would not be my last day. I kicked harder. I found strength where none should have existed.

I heard voices. I thought it was Jesus was calling me. The sun was glaring into my eyes. I took one last look up into the white light and saw a big orange float and heard the words "Grab the line." I barely had the strength remaining, but I reached for it. I heard Michelle surface next to me. "Are you alright?" she asked. I didn't have the strength left to answer. A crew member was pulling me back to the boat. I grabbed the ladder and tried to walk up, but my legs were like rubber and no longer working. Not only could I feel my heart pounding, I could see it. Things went black for a second. I waited for a moment until my vision came back, then with the help of the crew I slowly made my way up the ladder.

They sat me down and started taking my gear off. I felt sick, but as each piece of equipment was removed, I began to feel better. I stood up and removed the top part of my wetsuit. I finally felt okay, not good, but okay. Someone brought me a bottle of water and I guzzled it down. My heart was still pounding. That would take several minutes to subside.

Michelle made it back to the boat as well. She was in better condition than I. Swimming beneath the waves eliminated much of the difficulty. She sat down next to me and asked what was wrong. I looked at her and in one long rambling sentence said "I just swam the length of a football field, against a current, in a farmer John, on the surface, in four foot waves on a ninety degree day, carrying a spear gun, what the hell do you think is wrong? I'm nauseous, I'm tired, my hearts pounding out of my chest, I'm dehydrated and I didn't spear any damn fish! "

To say I was miserable would be an understatement. I was so miserable; I had no interest in getting back in the water for the second dive. In fact, I had already made the decision I was never diving again, period!

One by one my fellow divers came to speak with me. They all knew this was my first open ocean dive. One by one they worked to convince me to get back in the water. One told me to leave the spear gun on the boat. Another suggested adding a few more pounds of weight. The suggestions just kept coming. In the end there was one guy who motivated me to get back in the water. He walked over, sat down next to me, and asked "If you're not going to dive anymore, can I have your gear?" Up until that moment I had been vacillating back and forth between doing the second dive or not. I made my decision just minutes before the second dive, I was in.

I added a few pounds of weight and left the spear gun on the boat. I was not giving away my gear. Michelle promised to hold my hand during the dive and I kept her to that promise. We swam a large part of the dive holding hands. I enjoyed the dive and thanked Michelle and all my companions for pushing me back into the water. If I had not made that decision, I could not have written this book. The entire experience of that first day ignited my passion and the flame still burns.

On a side note, I learned something about spear fishing on this trip that I'd like to share with you. After returning to the boat from the second dive, while sitting on the back of the boat, one of my fellow divers popped up behind the boat with a spear shaft through the middle of his hand. It turns out he had lost the loading block for his pneumatic spear gun while he was underwater and rather than forget spear fishing or perhaps ask a fellow diver if he could borrow theirs, he picked up a clamshell and attempted to reload his gun using the clamshell as a block. The clamshell broke and the spear shaft went clear through the palm of his hand. He had a long and painful boat ride back to shore with a spear shaft through his hand. The lesson here is, do not use clamshells to reload pneumatic spear guns!

HAPPY ENDING

I had worked all morning scrubbing dirty, filthy boat bottoms when I returned to my truck and checked my voicemail. There was a message from a distraught young woman saying she really needed my help. The message went on to say that she had lost her engagement ring in the harbor while eating crabs at Captain Milo's restaurant.

I knew the location and I knew the water in that area was murky at best and quite nasty. It was full of debris from the restaurant and bad boaters. The bottom was littered with everything from glass bottles to aluminum cans, knives, forks, old rope and more. I almost didn't call her back, but I wasn't far from the location and hey, I was going to make my one hundred twenty five dollars whether I found the ring or not, so I returned her call.

The young lady had many questions, but through them all, one thing was certain - she really wanted to find that ring. I agreed to meet her at the restaurant in one hour.

Alan and I headed to the location. The owners of the restaurant were three old-timer brothers from Greece. They met with us upon our arrival and showed us approximately where they thought the ring might be. They had been there the night before when the girl lost the ring and had given us permission to come onto the property before normal business hours to conduct the search.

The young woman showed up with her husband and they met us on the dock. She verified the estimated location and I shook my head. This was not going to be an easy search. The ring had dropped between open grates on the dock and was underneath the restaurant deck. There was no way of knowing what I'd run into under there. It was a hazardous undertaking just to swim under the deck. The good news was that the water was shallow, about six feet, but that was the only good news.

I knew that if I had any chance of finding this ring, I could not touch the bottom. While I had an estimated location to start the search, the structure under the pier would have bounced the ring around like a pinball on the way down. In addition, touching the soft silt bottom would cause an immediate loss of visibility. I descended slowly, head first, keeping my feet (and fins) away from the bottom. From my inverted position the bottom came into view. I had roughly twelve inches of visibility to start. I began looking around. One of the first things I saw appeared to be a tab from a soda can. While I knew it could also be the bottom loop of a ring, I passed it by, not wanting to touch the bottom so soon into the search, sending the visibility to zero. I gingerly moved about, seeing all sorts of bottles, pieces of wood, plastic bags and metal pipes. Nothing else I saw had the potential to be a ring.

I headed back to the target and gently used my thumb and index finger to pluck the target from the silt. The mud billowed up like the cloud from the Hiroshima bomb blast. I couldn't see a thing. It is truly amazing how such a dainty pluck of something so small from a silted bottom can have such a dramatic effect.

I held the item up to my face and couldn't see it. I pressed it against my mask and still could not see it. I fanned the silt away from my face and waited… and waited. Suddenly the silt cleared and there it was, staring back at me - a huge beautiful diamond. I was so excited I couldn't wait to get it to the surface.

When my head broke the surface of the water, three or four voices all in unison asked "did you find it?" "Yep," I said… "I believe I did."

I passed it up to Alan and told him to ask the young lady if that was the ring she was looking for, as if there would have been any other diamond rings in that exact location. From beneath the deck I could hear the excitement in her voice as she exclaimed "Oh my God, I can't believe he found it!" I could hear her jumping up and down on the deck. From a completely different direction I heard "that's amazing." I looked up to see a guy fishing from a kayak. He gave me the thumbs up and I smiled back at him – "that's how you make a woman happy" I told him.

I scrambled out of the water to meet with my client and her hubby. I found out they had just been married the day before and had visited the restaurant for some famous Maryland blue crabs after finishing up at their wedding reception.

She and her husband took turns describing how the ring had been lost. Apparently she had taken the ring off to keep from getting "crabs all over it," and as she was putting it on her necklace for safe keeping, it slipped from her hands and went down into the clink. Her husband went on to inform me that it was a twenty-five thousand dollar ring and that while he was worried about the loss, the ring was insured. The girl chimed in, "Yeah, I could have had it replaced, but it wouldn't have been the one he gave me." She was so charmingly sentimental.

She asked if she could give me a big hug. I looked at her husband and said "Only if he says its' okay." He laughed and said "Sure." I got a big happy hug that day and she got her ring back. I know that diamonds are a girls' best friend, but divers who recover them are a close second!

The three Greek brothers who owned the restaurant invited Alan and I to come for crabs' on them. One of them then pulled me aside and whispered "You crazy, if I find that ring, I would keep it!" I think he was kidding. We had a good laugh and everyone went on their way. For me, I was just happy my day was done, but for that newlywed couple, well, one way or another, they had a happy ending.

THE TRAVELS OF KEN BARRICK (DIVE LOCATIONS)

UNITED STATES
Bainbridge, PA (Bainbridge quarry)
Delta, PA (Guppy Gulch quarry)
Willow Springs, PA (Willow Springs quarry)
Haymarket, VA (Millbrook quarry)
Baltimore, MD (Inner Harbor)
Ocean City, MD (Fenwick Shoals & wrecks)
Atlantic Beach, NC (The Graveyard of the Atlantic)
St. Lawrence River (Thousand Islands – New York Side)
San Diego, CA (Coronado Islands)

OUTISIDE THE UNITED STATES
Roatan, Honduras
Utila, Honduras
Curacao, Netherlands Antilles
Bonaire, Netherlands Antilles
Sea of Cortez – Cabo San Lucas, Mexico
Truk Lagoon, Federated States of Micronesia
Coral Sea & Great Barrier Reef, Cairns Australia
San Salvador Island, Bahamas
Bimini, Bahamas
The Exuma Islands, Bahamas
Little Cayman & Cayman Brac, Cayman Islands

ACKNOWLEDGEMENTS

I've always had an unexplained connection with the ocean. I think it began with my father taking me fishing when I was very young. The family trips to Ocean City, MD and central and south Florida further drove my budding interest in the sea. Learning to swim at a young age didn't hurt; it gave me confidence to step into the crashing waves at the waters' edge. My mom and dad built a swimming pool in the backyard and I spent countless hours in it each summer. In Florida, my Aunt Charlotte and Uncle Earl had alligators in their backyard, and they, along with my parents, would take me shark fishing on the beach. In addition, I became an avid crabber, in both Maryland and Florida. Credit should also be given to my uncle Will, who took me fishing, and my older cousins Diane and Russell, who were often with us during our Florida excursions.

Books, movies and television also played a role in developing my interest in the ocean. I remember watching Jacques Cousteau's underwater adventures and television series such as Sea Hunt. Early movies such as 20,000 Leagues under the Sea and Ghost Diver, together with later books turned movies such as Jaws, all contributed to my interest. If a book or movie was released about the ocean, I wanted to immerse myself in it.

It wasn't until I met Michelle that I fulfilled a life's dream. Somehow during my twenties I had shifted away from my love for the ocean. I still took my annual vacation to Ocean City, Maryland, and spent time on the beach, fishing and bodysurfing, but I was no longer enthralled with the sea. Perhaps I had come to take it for granted? Michelle changed all that when she bought me the SSI Open Water Scuba Diver course as a gift. I was going to become a SCUBA diver and be granted access to the underwater world in an unprecedented way. My life would be changed forever.

Over the years I've met many people in the diving industry. Some famous, some not so famous, but many of them have influenced me or increased my pleasure in the sport in some way, and I'd like to acknowledge them here. My first SCUBA Instructor was Martin Aldred. Martin taught me everything I needed to know to be a safe and competent diver. Then there is Thilo Glueck, who made diving fun and taught me how to be prepared for anything above or below the waterline. Bobby Edwards and Renate Eichenger of the *Atlantis IV,* for providing some of the best diving experiences the world has to offer.

I could go on and on about people who've made me laugh over the years, amazing travel companions, who made all the trips more fun. To all of my friends and fellow divers, I thank you all for touching my life in some way.

NOTES & BIBLIOGRAPHY

El Matador
1. Bitezones.com, *Shark Attacks of the Atlantic Ocean and The Gulf of Mexico* – Print
2. *10 Deadliest Sharks* Television Show – run from 2006 – 2011 on Discovery Channel

Re-living Operation Hailstorm
1. *Hailstorm Over Truk Lagoon: Operations Against Truk by Carrier Task Force 58, 17 and 18 February 1944, and Shipwrecks of World War II* by Klaus Lindemann.
2. *Peanuts and Pig Pen*, a Syndicated Cartoon and Cartoon Character by Charles Schulz

Proteus 8-17-2010
1. *Shipwrecks: Diving the Graveyard of the Atlantic* by Roderick M. Farb

ABOUT THE AUTHOR

1967 -

A child was born 8/22/1967 in Washington D.C. He was placed for adoption with Catholic Charities as an infant and was quickly adopted by Jack and Lorraine Barrick of Baltimore, MD., and given the name Kenneth. Ken has a younger brother Jeff and younger sister Michelle. He attended Woodlawn High before spending three years at Towson State University. In 1999 he married Michelle Christine Susa of Greensburg, PA. Michelle is largely credited for getting him started on his SCUBA diving adventures. He founded KB Diver Services, Inc. in 2002 and Off the Wall Scuba Inc. in 2007. Aside from writing this book, he published several issues of a small literary magazine – "Critique" from 1997 – 1999. He is an active SCUBA Instructor, dive business owner and recreational diver.